WE ARE KINGS AND PRIESTS

Dr. Maxwell Shimba

TABLE OF CONTENTS

INTRODUCTION

The Bible reveals a profound truth that believers in Christ are called to be both kings and priests in God's kingdom. This identity is not just symbolic; it embodies our purpose, calling, and relationship with God. Throughout Scripture, we see this concept of kingship and priesthood given as an essential part of God's plan, beginning in the Old Testament, continuing through the life and ministry of Jesus, and fulfilled in the New Testament church. To fully appreciate this unique calling, we must understand the historical and theological roots of kingship and priesthood, as well as what it means for our lives today.

The Concept of Kingship

Kingship in the Bible often denotes authority, governance, and the responsibility of caring for and leading God's people. The role of a king was not only about power; it was a sacred duty requiring wisdom, justice, and service. In ancient Israel, kings were chosen and anointed by God to act as His representatives, leading the people in righteousness and protecting them from enemies. Figures like King David and King Solomon represent this ideal of the divinely anointed leader, even though they, too, were flawed human beings who needed God's grace and guidance.

For believers, kingship is not about earthly political power but about spiritual authority. Through Christ, we are granted authority to reign in life, not as worldly rulers but as ambassadors of God's kingdom. Our kingship calls us to live lives marked by integrity, compassion, and purpose, exercising influence that reflects God's values and transforming our communities for the better. The concept of kingship is woven into the Christian life, reminding us that we are here to bring God's order, love, and peace to a broken world.

The Concept of Priesthood

In the Bible, the priesthood is a divine calling to represent people before God and to represent God to the people. The priests of Israel, particularly those from the tribe of Levi, served in the tabernacle and temple, performing sacrifices, maintaining worship practices, and interceding for the nation. Their primary responsibilities were rooted in holiness, atonement, and service. Priests acted as mediators between God and humanity, carrying out rituals that symbolized purification, forgiveness, and reconciliation with God.

This priestly role, however, was not meant to be limited to a select group. In Exodus 19:6, God declares to the entire nation of Israel, "You shall be to Me a kingdom of priests and a holy nation." Here, God reveals His desire for all His people to share in this role of service, worship, and intercession. In the New Testament, the apostle Peter extends this calling to all believers, calling us a royal priesthood, a holy nation (1 Peter 2:9). Through Christ's sacrifice and resurrection, believers now have direct access to God and are called to serve as priests, bringing others into God's presence through prayer, acts of service, and a life of worship.

Kings and Priests in Christ

The ultimate model of kingship and priesthood is found in Jesus Christ. Jesus is both the King of Kings and the High Priest, perfectly fulfilling both roles. As King, He reigns over all creation with justice, love, and truth. His kingdom is not earthly but spiritual, calling people from every nation and background into a new way of life. As Priest, He offered Himself as the ultimate sacrifice, bridging the gap between God and humanity and providing a way for us to enter into God's presence. In Christ, kingship and priesthood converge, showing us that true leadership is rooted in sacrificial love and that service to God and others is central to our calling.

Through our relationship with Jesus, we are empowered to live out our identity as both kings and priests. We are called to exercise authority over sin, death, and darkness, standing firm in our faith and influencing others for God's kingdom. At the same time, we are called to serve humbly, intercede for others, and live in holiness. These roles are not contradictory; they are complementary, reflecting the very nature of God's kingdom.

This book aims to explore the biblical foundation, historical context, and practical implications of our calling as kings and priests. By examining key Scriptures, we will see how this identity was foreshadowed in the Old Testament, fulfilled in Christ, and extended to all believers. Each chapter will dive into different aspects of what it means to reign with Christ and serve as His priests, offering practical insights for applying these truths in our daily lives.

As you journey through this book, be open to seeing yourself in a new light—as a royal priesthood, set apart for a divine purpose. Embracing this identity can transform your life, your relationships, and your community. It is my hope that you will be inspired to live out your calling with confidence and commitment, knowing that God has empowered you to make a lasting impact in His kingdom.

Purpose of the Book "We Are Kings and Priests"

The purpose of We Are Kings and Priests is to provide believers with a clear, in-depth understanding of their God-given identity and calling as both kings and priests in His kingdom. This book explores the biblical foundations of this dual role, examining how it has been progressively revealed throughout Scripture, fulfilled in Jesus Christ, and now entrusted to every believer.

Through this book, readers are invited to see the implications of their royal and priestly identity, not only as a theological concept but as a transformative reality that shapes their daily lives. By understanding kingship, readers can recognize the authority given to them through Christ to influence, lead, and overcome spiritual challenges. Likewise, through an understanding of priesthood, they can see the sacred calling to live a life of holiness, service, and intercession.

We Are Kings and Priests seeks to bridge the historical and the practical, giving believers the knowledge, encouragement, and inspiration to embrace their unique roles in God's plan. Through exploring key biblical texts, practical applications, and reflective questions, this book equips readers to step confidently into their divine calling, to lead and serve with purpose, and to participate in God's mission in the world.

xi

DR. MAXWELL SHIMBA

CHAPTER 01

BIBLICAL FOUNDATIONS OF KINGS AND PRIESTS

Revelation 1:6-9

The opening chapter of the book of Revelation, penned by the apostle John, introduces a profound truth about the identity of believers: they are made both kings and priests unto God through Jesus Christ. This declaration, found in Revelation 1:6, forms the biblical foundation for understanding the dual role that every follower of Christ is called to live out.

The apostle John, in Revelation 1:6-9, underlines the immense privilege and responsibility bestowed upon believers. This passage tells us that it is through Jesus Christ's redemptive work that we are given a new identity—an identity marked by royal authority and priestly service. These two roles, which in ancient Israel were often separate, are now combined for every believer.

The King's Authority

To be a king in God's kingdom means to exercise spiritual authority and dominion. Jesus, the King of Kings, shares His authority with us, enabling us to overcome the power of sin, darkness, and evil in this world. This kingship is not about ruling over others in a worldly sense but is instead a call to reign in life by the power of the Holy Spirit. As Romans 5:17 says, through Christ, we are empowered to "reign in life." This authority is manifested in the believer's ability to walk in victory, to make righteous decisions, and to influence the world around them for the kingdom of God.

A believer's kingship is also a reflection of their divine inheritance. As sons and daughters of God, we are heirs to His kingdom, endowed with spiritual rights and responsibilities. We are called to govern our lives and actions with godly wisdom, leading others by example and using our authority to establish God's will on earth.

The Priest's Service

In addition to kingship, believers are called to be priests. The role of a priest is primarily one of service to God and others. Priests in the Old Testament stood as mediators between God and the people, offering sacrifices and prayers on behalf of the nation. Today, as priests in the New Covenant, believers no longer offer animal sacrifices but spiritual sacrifices—praise, worship, prayer, and intercession (1 Peter 2:5).

The priestly role is one of intercession and holiness. It calls for believers to live lives set apart for God's service, offering up their lives as living sacrifices (Romans 12:1). We are called to be channels through which others can come to know God, to pray on their behalf, and to stand in the gap as intercessors. In this sense, the priesthood is marked by love and compassion, always seeking to reconcile people to God.

The Dual Role in God's Kingdom

The combination of these two roles—king and priest—forms a powerful identity for every believer. As kings, we have authority and dominion to establish God's will, and as priests, we have the responsibility to serve, pray, and intercede for others. In Revelation 1:6, John makes it clear that this identity is not just reserved for a select few but is the inheritance of all who believe in Christ.

By making us kings and priests, God has entrusted us with both power and purpose. As kings, we are to walk in the authority of His kingdom, bringing heaven's influence into the earth. As priests, we are to live holy, sacrificial lives, ministering to others and bringing them closer to God. This dual role is essential to understanding our place in God's redemptive plan for humanity.

Revelation 5:10: A Further Emphasis

To further understand this identity, we can look at another passage in the book of Revelation. In Revelation 5:10, the heavenly chorus sings about the redeemed, declaring, "You have made them to be a kingdom and priests to serve our God, and they will reign on the earth." This passage reinforces the truth that believers are both kings and priests and that this identity is central to their purpose on earth. It highlights that this royal priesthood is not just a spiritual concept but has a practical outworking in the world today.

As we embrace our calling as kings and priests, we step into the fullness of our God-given potential. Through this dual role, we participate in the unfolding of God's kingdom, bringing His light, love, and justice into a world that desperately needs it. This is the high calling of every believer—a royal priesthood, called to reign with Christ and serve His purpose for all eternity.

In the subsequent chapters, we will explore the biblical history and development of this royal priesthood, its significance in the life of Jesus, and how we as believers can live out this calling in every aspect of our lives today.

Biblical Foundation of Kings and Priests according to Exodus 19:6

Exodus 19:6 is a foundational verse that lays the groundwork for the concept of a royal priesthood in the Bible. In this verse, God speaks directly to Moses on Mount Sinai, declaring, "And you shall be to Me a kingdom of priests and a holy nation." This verse carries immense significance, not just for ancient Israel but for all believers, as it unveils God's desire for His people to serve as both kings and priests.

This covenantal promise was given at a pivotal moment in Israel's history. After the Israelites were delivered from slavery in Egypt and brought to Mount Sinai, God entered into a formal covenant with them. He proclaimed that if they obeyed His voice and kept His covenant, they would become His treasured possession among all nations. Exodus 19:6 was part of this divine promise, where God set the Israelites apart for a special purpose.

A Kingdom of Priests

The phrase "kingdom of priests" implies that Israel was called to serve both as royal representatives of God's authority and as priests who mediated between God and humanity. In ancient Israel, kings ruled with authority, but priests were charged with upholding the spiritual life of the nation. However, in Exodus 19:6, God blends these two roles together, describing the entire nation of Israel as a priestly kingdom.

As priests, Israel's role was not just limited to religious rituals but extended to representing God's holiness and mediating His presence to the surrounding nations. Israel was called to be a living example of what it meant to be in covenant with God. They were to declare His glory to the nations, acting as spiritual ambassadors who revealed God's nature, laws, and justice to the world. This priestly calling reflected God's desire for His people to be instruments of His blessing, offering spiritual sacrifices and leading others into relationship with Him.

A Holy Nation

In addition to being a kingdom of priests, God also declared that Israel would be a "holy nation." Holiness, in biblical terms, means being set apart for a sacred purpose. For Israel, this meant living according to God's laws and reflecting His moral character in every aspect of their lives. Holiness was not just a matter of personal piety but a national identity that was meant to set them apart from other nations.

As a holy nation, Israel was called to embody God's righteousness, justice, and mercy. Their distinct way of life—defined by obedience to God's commandments, their worship practices, and their treatment of others—was to serve as a testimony to the nations around them. This holiness would allow Israel to fulfill its role as a kingdom of priests, showing the world what it looked like to live under God's reign.

The Purpose of the Covenant

Exodus 19:6 reveals the purpose of the covenant that God established with Israel. This covenant wasn't just about forming a special relationship between God and His people— it was about creating a nation that would serve a global purpose. By being a kingdom of priests and a holy nation, Israel was to stand as a beacon of God's light in the midst of a dark and fallen world. They were chosen not only to be God's people but also to be His representatives, showing the nations what it meant to serve the living God.

This covenantal calling highlights a key theme in the Bible: God's desire for His people to partner with Him in His redemptive plan for the world. By calling Israel a kingdom of priests and a holy nation, God set in motion a plan that would ultimately culminate in Jesus Christ and extend to all who believe in Him.

The Priestly Role in the New Testament

The idea of a kingdom of priests introduced in Exodus 19:6 is later picked up in the New Testament, especially in 1 Peter 2:9, where the church is described as a "chosen people, a royal priesthood, a holy nation, God's special possession." The promise that was once given to Israel is now extended to all believers through Christ. In Christ, the royal priesthood is fulfilled, and the church is called to continue the priestly work of representing God to the world.

Just as Israel was called to reflect God's holiness and serve as spiritual mediators, so too is the church today called to live holy lives and proclaim the gospel of Jesus Christ. Through this calling, believers participate in the mission that began with Israel at Mount Sinai, but which now reaches its fulfillment through the new covenant established by Jesus' death and resurrection.

Exodus 19:6 serves as a powerful reminder that God has always desired for His people to play a pivotal role in His plan for the world. The call to be a kingdom of priests and a holy nation is not just a matter of privilege but of responsibility. It is a calling to live set-apart lives that reflect God's character and to serve as mediators, bringing others into His kingdom.

As we move forward, we will see how this theme is developed further in Scripture and what it means for us as believers today, living as kings and priests in God's kingdom.

Biblical Foundation of Kings and Priests according to 1 Peter 2:9-12

In 1 Peter 2:9-12, the apostle Peter emphasizes the identity and calling of believers in Christ by reiterating the theme of a royal priesthood. Just as Israel was chosen to be a kingdom of priests and a holy nation in Exodus 19:6, Peter applies this same divine calling to the church. This passage not only affirms the special identity of Christians but also highlights their role and purpose in the world. Peter writes, "But you are a chosen people, a royal priesthood, a holy nation, God's special possession, that you may declare the praises of Him who called you out of darkness into His wonderful light."

A Chosen People

Peter begins by addressing believers as a "chosen people," affirming that their identity is rooted in God's sovereign election. Just as Israel was chosen by God to fulfill His purposes, the church, made up of people from all nations, is now God's chosen instrument to carry out His mission in the world. This choice is not based on personal merit or human achievement but solely on God's grace and love. By choosing His people, God has set them apart for a special purpose—one that involves both kingship and priesthood.

The idea of being "chosen" also implies a relationship with God that is deeply personal and covenantal. Believers are God's treasured possession, drawn into a relationship with

Him that involves intimate fellowship, divine favor, and participation in His work on earth. This chosen identity is foundational to understanding the role that believers play as royal priests.

A Royal Priesthood

The phrase "royal priesthood" directly connects believers to the dual roles of kings and priests. This royal priesthood combines the authority of kingship with the sacred responsibilities of the priesthood. As part of this royal priesthood, Christians are endowed with spiritual authority through Christ and are called to serve as intermediaries between God and the world.

As royal priests, believers are called to reign in life through the power of Christ (Romans 5:17), exercising dominion over sin and representing God's kingdom on earth. Simultaneously, their priestly role involves offering spiritual sacrifices, interceding on behalf of others, and living lives of holiness and service. This dual identity signifies both the privilege and the responsibility of being God's representatives in a broken world.

In ancient Israel, the roles of king and priest were typically separate, but in Christ, these roles are united. Jesus, as the ultimate King and High Priest, has made it possible for His followers to share in His kingship and priesthood.

Believers are now equipped to walk in authority while also serving as channels of God's grace and mercy.

A Holy Nation

Peter's description of the church as a "holy nation" echoes the language of Exodus 19:6, where Israel is called to be a holy nation set apart for God. Holiness, in this context, means to be consecrated to God's service, living in a way that reflects His character and values. The church, as a holy nation, is called to live differently from the world, embodying the righteousness, love, and justice of God.

Being a holy nation means that believers are distinct, not because of nationality or ethnic background, but because of their relationship with God. Their holiness is derived from their union with Christ, who has sanctified them by His sacrifice. This holiness is not just an abstract concept but is meant to be lived out practically, through obedience to God's Word, love for others, and a commitment to moral purity.

God's Special Possession

Peter goes on to describe believers as "God's special possession." This phrase highlights the deep value that God places on His people. Just as a king treasures his royal inheritance, God cherishes His people, regarding them as precious and irreplaceable. This image of being God's special possession is a reminder of the security and identity believers have in Him. They belong to God, and this belonging is eternal and unshakable.

Being God's special possession also means that believers are uniquely loved and protected by Him. It underscores the idea that Christians are not only saved from sin but also saved for a purpose—to glorify God and advance His kingdom on earth.

Declaring the Praises of God

The ultimate purpose of being a royal priesthood and a holy nation is to "declare the praises of Him who called you out of darkness into His wonderful light." This statement captures the heart of the believer's mission: to proclaim the greatness of God. The calling out of darkness and into light refers to the transformation that occurs when someone becomes a follower of Christ. Through Christ, believers are delivered from the spiritual darkness of sin, ignorance, and death, and brought into the light of salvation, truth, and eternal life.

This new identity compels believers to declare God's praises, both through worship and witness. As kings and priests, Christians are called to make known the character and works of God to the world. Their lives should reflect the goodness, mercy, and faithfulness of God, drawing others to experience the same salvation they have received.

Living as Aliens and Strangers in the World

In 1 Peter 2:11-12, Peter shifts from theological identity to practical exhortation. He urges believers to live as "aliens and strangers" in this world, abstaining from sinful desires and living lives that are honorable among unbelievers. This part of the passage emphasizes that the identity of being a royal priesthood comes with the responsibility of living in a way that reflects that calling.

Believers are called to live as citizens of heaven, not conforming to the patterns of this world. As a holy nation, their conduct should be distinct, marked by integrity, love, and righteousness. By living honorable lives, believers not only bring glory to God but also serve as a testimony to those who do not yet know Him. Peter highlights the importance of maintaining a witness that points others to Christ, even in the face of persecution or opposition.

Continuity and Fulfillment of the Old Testament Promise

The language Peter uses in this passage—chosen people, royal priesthood, holy nation—directly connects the church to the promises made to Israel in the Old Testament. The church, as the body of Christ, is the fulfillment of the covenantal calling given to Israel. Through Jesus, the blessings and promises once reserved for the nation of Israel are extended to all who believe in Him, Jew and Gentile alike.

This continuity between the Old and New Testaments underscores the unfolding of God's redemptive plan throughout history. The royal priesthood that began with Israel is now fully realized in Christ, and the church is the means through which God's kingdom is advanced in the world.

In 1 Peter 2:9-12, the apostle Peter invites believers to embrace their true identity as a royal priesthood and a holy nation, reminding them of their high calling and their purpose. They are chosen by God, set apart for His service, and called to declare His praises in the world. This passage not only reaffirms the continuity of the royal priesthood from the Old Testament but also challenges believers to live out this calling with integrity, holiness, and purpose in the present age.

In the next chapters, we will explore how this royal priesthood was embodied in the Old Testament and fulfilled in the person of Jesus Christ, as well as its practical implications for believers today.

CHAPTER 02

HISTORICAL CONTEXT OF KINGS AND PRIESTS IN ANCIENT ISRAEL

Role of Kings in Israel

In ancient Israel, the role of kings was central to the governance and well-being of the nation. The king was appointed to provide leadership, administer justice, and protect the people, particularly in times of conflict and war. Though the Israelites initially operated under a theocracy with God as their direct ruler, they eventually demanded a king, as seen in 1 Samuel 8:5, where the elders of Israel asked the prophet Samuel, "Now appoint a king to lead us, such as all the other nations have."

Kingship in Israel was a mix of divine mandate and human responsibility, with the king acting as God's representative on earth. The king's success or failure had direct implications for the spiritual and social state of the nation. Kings like David and Solomon are two prime examples of leadership in Israel's history, and their reigns help illuminate both the strengths and the weaknesses inherent in this role.

Governance and Justice

One of the primary responsibilities of kings in Israel was to govern the people with justice and righteousness. The king was expected to ensure the enforcement of God's laws and to maintain social order. Kings were often described as sitting in judgment, making decisions on legal matters, and resolving disputes. Psalm 72 offers a prayer for the king, asking that he judge the people righteously and bring justice to the afflicted. This psalm reflects the king's responsibility to be a protector of the weak, the poor, and those who were oppressed.

While the king held significant authority, he was ultimately subject to God's law. The ideal king in Israel was expected to lead in accordance with divine instructions, ensuring that justice and righteousness prevailed throughout the land. The standard for this type of governance is perhaps best exemplified in Deuteronomy 17:18-20, which instructs the king to write a copy of the law for himself and to study it throughout his reign. This act was meant to remind the king that his authority was derivative and that his reign should reflect God's will and purpose.

Military Leadership

Kings in ancient Israel were also expected to lead the people in military battles and defend the nation against external threats. The king's role as a warrior-leader was crucial in maintaining national security and asserting Israel's dominance over its enemies. Many kings in Israel, especially in the early monarchy, were known for their military exploits. King Saul, Israel's first king, was chosen largely for his ability to lead the people in battle against the Philistines (1 Samuel 9:16).

Perhaps the most famous military king was David, who rose to prominence after his victory over the giant Goliath and later became king of Israel. David's reign was marked by numerous military successes, including the consolidation of Israel's territories and the defeat of surrounding enemies. His military achievements were not only important for the security of the nation but also for the establishment of Israel as a regional power.

However, military success alone did not define the kingship. While victory in battle was important, the kings were also judged by how closely they aligned themselves with God's will. When kings relied on their own strength and failed to seek divine guidance, their military endeavors often ended in failure, as seen in the reigns of several later kings who neglected their relationship with God.

Divine Anointing and Guidance

Although kings in Israel were given authority to rule, their reigns were meant to be under the direct guidance and sovereignty of God. This divine mandate was often symbolized by the act of anointing, where a prophet or priest would anoint the king with oil, signifying God's approval and blessing. For example, the prophet Samuel anointed both Saul and David as kings of Israel (1 Samuel 10:1, 1 Samuel 16:13).

The anointing of a king was not merely a ceremonial act but also a reminder that the king's authority came from God and was to be exercised in accordance with His commands. The king's success was tied to his faithfulness to God's covenant, and any deviation from that covenant could result in disastrous consequences for both the king and the nation. For instance, Saul's disobedience to God's instructions ultimately led to his downfall and the transfer of the kingdom to David (1 Samuel 15:26-28).

Kings like Solomon, who began their reigns with divine wisdom and guidance, also provide insight into the importance of maintaining a relationship with God. Solomon's wisdom, which was a direct gift from God (1

Kings 3:5-14), enabled him to lead the nation with great prosperity and peace during the early part of his reign. However, later in life, Solomon's departure from God's laws, particularly his involvement in idolatry and foreign alliances, led to the decline of his kingdom (1 Kings 11:1-11). This underscores the constant need for divine guidance and the perils of kings relying solely on their own understanding.

Human Flaws and Failures

Despite the divinely ordained role of kings, the history of Israel's monarchy reveals the profound human flaws of many of its leaders. Even revered kings like David had significant moral failures. David, though known as a man after God's own heart, committed grievous sins, including adultery with Bathsheba and the orchestrated death of her husband Uriah (2 Samuel 11). While David repented and sought God's forgiveness, the consequences of his actions reverberated throughout his reign, leading to turmoil within his own family and the kingdom.

Similarly, King Solomon, who began his reign with unmatched wisdom and favor from God, fell into idolatry and moral compromise by the end of his life, largely because of his many foreign wives and their influence over him (1 Kings 11:4-6). This serves as a reminder that even the most blessed and gifted leaders are susceptible to failure when they neglect their relationship with God.

Other kings, such as King Ahab, represent some of the darkest chapters in Israel's monarchy. Ahab, under the influence of his wife Jezebel, promoted idol worship, particularly of Baal, and oppressed the prophets of God. His reign is marked by violence, moral decay, and rebellion against God's commandments, leading to eventual judgment upon him and his house (1 Kings 16:30-33).

The Need for Divine Leadership

The history of Israel's kings ultimately highlights the need for divine leadership and the limitations of human rulers. While some kings sought God's will and led with righteousness, many fell short, revealing that no earthly king could fully fulfill the role of a perfect ruler. This constant failure pointed to the need for a greater King—one who would reign in perfect justice, righteousness, and truth.

This need is fulfilled in Jesus Christ, who is both the King of Kings and the High Priest. Jesus embodies the ultimate ideal of kingship, ruling with wisdom, justice, and compassion, while also serving as a priest who intercedes on behalf of humanity. His reign is eternal and transcends the limitations of earthly rulers, bringing the perfect combination of authority and priestly service that the human kings of Israel could only foreshadow.

In the next section, we will explore the role of priests in ancient Israel, focusing on their duties, their relationship with the kings, and how their priesthood set the stage for the New Testament understanding of the believer's role as a priest unto God.

Role of Priests in Israel

The role of priests in ancient Israel was vital to the religious and spiritual life of the nation. Priests were responsible for mediating between God and the people, performing sacrifices, maintaining the sacred space of the temple, and leading the people in worship. Their work was essential to maintaining Israel's covenant relationship with God, ensuring that the nation remained spiritually connected to Him through ritual purity, sacrifice, and intercession.

The priesthood was established from the tribe of Levi, with the family of Aaron—Moses' brother—specifically chosen for the high priestly duties. The Levites were set apart for the sacred service of the tabernacle and later the temple, acting as the mediators of God's presence among His people. This system of priesthood and the priestly duties they performed were crucial to Israel's identity as a holy nation.

Performing Sacrifices

One of the central responsibilities of the priests was to offer sacrifices on behalf of the people. Sacrifices were an essential aspect of Israel's worship and relationship with God. These sacrifices were offered for various reasons, including the atonement of sin, thanksgiving, and covenantal offerings. The sacrificial system is detailed primarily in the Book of Leviticus, which outlines the specific offerings that priests were required to perform, such as burnt offerings, sin offerings, peace offerings, and grain offerings.

Each type of sacrifice had its own purpose:

- Burnt offerings were made to atone for the general sinfulness of the people and to symbolize their devotion to God.

- Sin offerings were for specific sins that individuals or the nation committed, seeking forgiveness and reconciliation with God.

- Peace offerings symbolized fellowship with God, expressing gratitude or fulfilling a vow.

- Grain offerings were non-blood sacrifices made as an offering of thanksgiving to God.

The act of sacrifice was the primary means by which the people of Israel could atone for their sins and maintain a relationship with God. Priests acted as the intermediaries who offered these sacrifices on behalf of individuals and the nation. Their role was essential because they ensured that the proper rites were performed in accordance with the laws given by God, ensuring that sin was dealt with in a way that upheld the holiness of God and His covenant.

Maintaining the Temple

Priests were also responsible for maintaining the tabernacle during the time of the wilderness wanderings and later the Temple in Jerusalem. The tabernacle, and subsequently the temple, were considered the dwelling place of God's presence on earth, and the priests were entrusted with the care of this sacred space. Their duties included ensuring that the rituals, such as the lighting of the lamps, the burning of incense, and the offering of the sacrifices, were carried out properly.

In addition to performing their duties, priests had to ensure that the temple remained ritually pure. This meant they followed strict purity laws regarding cleanliness, food, and other ritualistic practices. Any violation of the sacredness of the temple would result in the defilement of the space and could jeopardize Israel's covenant relationship with God. As such, the priests were tasked with a heavy responsibility—protecting and maintaining the sanctity of the dwelling place of the Almighty.

The high priest, the chief among the priests, had an even more sacred role. Only the high priest could enter the Holy of Holies, the most sacred part of the temple, and this could only be done once a year on Yom Kippur, the Day of Atonement. On this day, the high priest made atonement for the sins of the nation, offering sacrifices and sprinkling blood on the Ark of the Covenant to seek God's mercy and forgiveness.

Intercession on Behalf of the People

Priests served as intercessors between God and the people, praying for the nation and seeking God's favor on their behalf. This role of intercession was closely tied to their work of offering sacrifices, as the priests pleaded with God for the forgiveness and restoration of Israel. Intercession was a key part of their function, as it ensured that the people remained in right standing with God.

One of the most significant examples of priestly intercession is found in Numbers 16, when the rebellion of Korah and his followers resulted in divine judgment against Israel. When a plague began to spread among the people, Aaron the high priest took a censer filled with incense and ran into the midst of the congregation to make atonement for the people, standing "between the dead and the living" (Numbers 16:48). His act of intercession stopped the plague and saved many lives. This illustrates the critical role that priests played in mediating between God's judgment and the people's sin.

In addition to corporate intercession, priests were responsible for individual intercessions. When individuals brought their sacrifices to the tabernacle or temple, it was the priest's duty to present the offering before God and ensure that the individual received the necessary atonement and blessing. This personal aspect of the priesthood made the priests accessible to the people, ensuring that their spiritual needs were met.

Teaching the Law

In addition to their ritual and intercessory duties, priests also had the responsibility to teach the people God's law. They were considered the custodians of the divine commandments and were expected to instruct the people in the ways of righteousness. Leviticus 10:11 explicitly commands the priests to "teach the children of Israel all the statutes which the Lord has spoken." Their teaching role ensured that the nation remained aware of the covenant requirements and that future generations would continue to walk in God's ways.

Priests often served as judges in legal disputes, using their knowledge of the law to settle conflicts and ensure justice. This further elevated their role in society as they not only dealt with the spiritual life of Israel but also played a vital role in the administration of justice and governance, alongside the kings. Their influence extended beyond the temple, as they provided spiritual guidance and moral instruction to the people.

The Levitical Priesthood and the Covenant

The priesthood, particularly the Levites, were at the heart of Israel's covenant relationship with God. Their work in the temple and their service in teaching the law ensured that Israel remained faithful to the covenant that God established with them at Mount Sinai. Without the priests, the people's ability to maintain holiness and to approach God would have been severely diminished.

The Levitical priesthood was a symbol of God's desire for His people to be a kingdom of priests and a holy nation, a calling that was not just for the tribe of Levi but for all of Israel. However, the priestly system revealed the limitations of human mediators and the imperfection of sacrifices made by men. The priests, while essential to maintaining the covenant, were themselves flawed and required their own atonement for sin.

This points to the need for a greater priesthood, one that would not require continual sacrifices and imperfect mediators. In the New Testament, this need is fulfilled in the person of Jesus Christ, who serves as the ultimate High Priest, according to the order of Melchizedek (Hebrews 7). Jesus' sacrifice is perfect, once and for all, removing the need for the Levitical system and opening the way for all believers to have direct access to God.

In the next section, we will explore the intersection of kingship and priesthood, examining how these roles complemented each other and ultimately point forward to the perfect King and High Priest, Jesus Christ. Through this examination, we will understand how the biblical model of kings and priests in ancient Israel serves as a foundation for the believer's identity today as both kings and priests unto God.

Intersection of Kingship and Priesthood

Although the roles of king and priest in ancient Israel were distinct, they both served an intertwined purpose—leading the people in faithfulness to God and ensuring the spiritual and societal well-being of the nation. Kings were responsible for governing the people with justice and defending the nation, while priests were charged with maintaining the spiritual life of the people, offering sacrifices, interceding, and teaching God's law. Together, these two offices played complementary roles in guiding Israel to live under the rule of God.

However, as we explore the biblical narrative, we find that while kingship and priesthood were meant to serve different functions, there were significant points of intersection where their roles overlapped. This intersection of kingship and priesthood finds its ultimate and perfect fulfillment in Jesus Christ, who is both the eternal King and High Priest. In Christ, the two offices are unified, bringing to fruition the ultimate purpose of leadership in God's kingdom.

The King's Responsibility for Spiritual Leadership

While the primary role of the king was political and judicial, kings in Israel were also expected to guide the people spiritually. Kings were not merely secular rulers but were meant to govern under God's divine authority, acting as His representatives on earth. They were responsible for ensuring that the people adhered to the covenant and that the nation remained faithful to God's commandments.

For example, King David, the archetype of Israel's kings, combined both political leadership and spiritual devotion. His leadership went beyond military and administrative functions; David also expressed a deep personal devotion to God, exemplified in the Psalms he wrote. His role as king included fostering worship and ensuring that the people followed the laws of God. Although he was not a priest, David's heart for God and his leadership in bringing the Ark of the Covenant to Jerusalem (2 Samuel 6) highlight the spiritual dimension of his kingship.

Similarly, King Solomon, David's son, was known not only for his wisdom but also for building the Temple in Jerusalem, the most important religious structure in Israel's history. This act linked Solomon's reign with the nation's spiritual life, demonstrating the king's responsibility for Israel's relationship with God. Though Solomon himself was not a priest, his actions had priestly significance, as he ensured that Israel had a permanent place of worship where sacrifices could be made, and God's presence could dwell among the people.

When the kings were faithful to God, the nation prospered spiritually. However, when kings fell into idolatry or neglected their spiritual duties, the entire nation suffered. Kings like Ahab and Manasseh led Israel into idol worship, which brought God's judgment upon the people. This further illustrates the king's role in maintaining the spiritual health of the nation, showing that kingship in Israel was deeply connected to priestly functions.

The Priest's Role in National Leadership

While the priests were primarily responsible for spiritual and religious duties, their influence extended into the realm of national leadership. Priests often acted as advisors to kings, providing guidance on matters of spiritual and political significance. For instance, Zadok the priest anointed King Solomon at the instruction of King David (1 Kings 1:39), emphasizing the priestly role in the transfer of royal authority.

Moreover, priests like Jehoiada played crucial roles in safeguarding the future of the monarchy. Jehoiada protected the young King Joash from being killed by Queen Athaliah and later guided him to rule in faithfulness to God (2 Kings 11). This close interaction between the priest and the king illustrates how the roles of spiritual and political leadership were intertwined.

Additionally, priests were instrumental in leading the people in repentance and returning them to God during times of national crisis. In moments of spiritual decline, the high priest would often work alongside the king to call the nation back to covenant faithfulness. For example, during the reign of King Hezekiah, the priests and Levites were crucial in the restoration of the temple and the re-establishment of proper worship after a period of widespread idolatry (2 Chronicles 29).

These examples demonstrate that while the king ruled politically and the priest ministered spiritually, both offices were deeply involved in guiding the nation toward its covenantal relationship with God. When the king and priest worked together harmoniously, the nation flourished both spiritually and politically.

The Merging of Kingship and Priesthood in the Messiah

While the roles of king and priest remained separate throughout much of Israel's history, the Hebrew Scriptures contained hints that one day these two offices would be unified in a future messianic figure. This expectation is seen in prophecies about the coming Messiah, who would be both a righteous King and a priestly figure who mediates between God and humanity.

The clearest foreshadowing of this merging of kingship and priesthood is found in the figure of Melchizedek, who appears briefly in Genesis 14. Melchizedek was both the king of Salem and a priest of God Most High. He blessed Abraham and received tithes from him, demonstrating both royal authority and priestly function. The author of Hebrews later identifies Melchizedek as a type of Christ, showing that Jesus' priesthood is according to the order of Melchizedek—eternal and unchangeable (Hebrews 7:1-17).

The prophet Zechariah also foretold the merging of these two offices in the coming Messiah. In Zechariah 6:12-13, the prophet speaks of a figure known as the Branch (a title for the Messiah), who would "build the temple of the Lord" and "sit and rule on His throne," and he would "be a priest on His throne." This prophecy points to a future time when the Messiah would combine the roles of king and priest in one person.

Jesus Christ: The Eternal King and High Priest

The ultimate fulfillment of the merging of kingship and priesthood is found in Jesus Christ. Jesus is both the eternal King, ruling over all creation, and the perfect High Priest, mediating between God and humanity. Through His life, death, and resurrection, Jesus accomplished what no earthly king or priest could—He brought eternal redemption and established a kingdom that would never end.

As King, Jesus reigns over the entire universe. He is the King of Kings and Lord of Lords (Revelation 19:16), and His rule is characterized by justice, righteousness, and peace. Unlike the flawed kings of Israel, Jesus' kingship is perfect and eternal. His authority is absolute, and His kingdom will never be shaken (Hebrews 12:28).

As High Priest, Jesus fulfills the priestly role by offering Himself as the ultimate sacrifice for sin. The book of

Hebrews emphasizes that Jesus' priesthood is superior to the Levitical priesthood because He offered a perfect and once-for-all sacrifice (Hebrews 9:11-14). Moreover, Jesus continually intercedes for believers, acting as the mediator between God and humanity (Hebrews 7:25).

In Jesus, we see the perfect union of the kingly and priestly offices. He governs with absolute authority, but He also serves with compassion and mercy. His reign is marked by both justice and grace, and His priestly intercession ensures that His people are eternally secure in their relationship with God.

Through His death and resurrection, Jesus has made all believers partakers in His kingship and priesthood. 1 Peter 2:9 declares that we are "a royal priesthood," called to reign with Christ and serve God's purposes on earth. Believers now share in the privileges of kingship—walking in spiritual authority—and in the responsibilities of priesthood—offering spiritual sacrifices and interceding for others.

In this chapter, we have explored how kingship and priesthood intersected in ancient Israel and how these roles are perfectly unified in Jesus Christ. The complementary nature of these two offices reveals God's design for leadership and spiritual guidance in His kingdom. In the chapters that follow, we will delve deeper into how believers can live out this royal priesthood in their daily lives, following the example set by Jesus, the eternal King and High Priest.

CHAPTER 03

THE ROYAL PRIESTHOOD IN THE OLD TESTAMENT

Genesis: The Beginning of the Priesthood

The concept of priesthood in the Old Testament has its origins as early as the book of Genesis, where we see glimpses of priestly roles even before the formal establishment of the Levitical priesthood. Two significant figures in Genesis—Adam and Melchizedek—serve as early models of priesthood, pointing toward the larger biblical theme of a royal priesthood that will eventually culminate in Jesus Christ.

Adam: The First Priest in the Garden of Eden

Although the word "priest" is not used in the description of Adam's life in the Garden of Eden, his role in creation bears priestly characteristics. Adam was given dominion over the earth, tasked with caring for the garden, and was placed in direct communion with God. These responsibilities and privileges parallel the later duties of priests, who were called to cultivate God's creation and maintain the sanctity of His presence.

In Genesis 2:15, God placed Adam in the Garden of Eden "to work it and keep it" (ESV). The Hebrew words used here for "work" (abad) and "keep" (shamar) are significant because they are later used in relation to the duties of the Levitical priests. In Numbers 3:7-8, for example, the Levites are tasked with "serving" (abad) in the tabernacle and "guarding" (shamar) its sacred space. Adam's role, therefore, can be understood as priestly, as he was responsible for maintaining the order and holiness of God's creation, much like the priests who later maintained the temple and its worship practices.

Moreover, Adam's direct relationship with God in the garden reflects the priestly role of mediating between God and creation. As the first human being, Adam was the original steward of God's presence on earth, walking with God in the cool of the day (Genesis 3:8). He had a unique access to God, symbolizing the ideal relationship between God and humanity—a relationship that later priests would seek to mediate on behalf of the people.

However, with Adam's fall into sin, this priestly role was fractured. The disruption of his communion with God due to sin foreshadows the need for a new priestly order that could restore the broken relationship between God and humanity. This need for restoration would later be fulfilled in the figure of Christ, who restores humanity to its original purpose as a royal priesthood.

Melchizedek: The King and Priest of Salem

The mysterious figure of Melchizedek, introduced in Genesis 14:18-20, provides one of the earliest and clearest examples of the merging of kingship and priesthood in the Old Testament. Melchizedek is described as the king of Salem (likely ancient Jerusalem) and a priest of God Most High. His dual role as both king and priest prefigures the eventual union of these offices in Jesus Christ, who is both the King of Kings and the eternal High Priest.

Melchizedek's encounter with Abraham occurs after Abraham's military victory over the kings who had captured his nephew Lot. As Abraham returns from battle, Melchizedek comes out to meet him, offering bread and wine and blessing Abraham. In return, Abraham gives Melchizedek a tithe—a tenth of all the spoils—recognizing Melchizedek's superior spiritual authority.

Several aspects of Melchizedek's priesthood are noteworthy:

1. His Royal Authority: As both king and priest, Melchizedek holds a position of great authority. His kingship over Salem suggests that he ruled a city known for peace (the name "Salem" is related to the Hebrew word for peace, "shalom"). This combination of royal and priestly functions foreshadows the perfect reign of Christ, who will bring eternal peace through His priestly intercession.

2. His Blessing of Abraham: Melchizedek's blessing of Abraham is significant because it demonstrates his role as a mediator between God and humanity. He blesses Abraham on behalf of God Most High, acknowledging that Abraham's victory in battle came through divine provision. This act of blessing aligns with the priestly function of mediating divine favor to the people.

3. His Offering of Bread and Wine: The offering of bread and wine by Melchizedek is symbolic and has been seen by many Christian theologians as a foreshadowing of the Eucharist (the Lord's Supper). In this act, Melchizedek's priesthood points to the sacrificial ministry of Christ, who would offer His own body and blood for the redemption of humanity.

4. A Priest of God Most High: Unlike the later Levitical priesthood, which was tied to the law of Moses and the descendants of Aaron, Melchizedek's priesthood was universal, not bound by lineage or tribal affiliation. He is described as a priest of "God Most High" (El Elyon), which emphasizes his priestly role as one that transcends national boundaries. This universal priesthood foreshadows the priesthood of Christ, who is not limited to a particular people but serves as the eternal High Priest for all nations.

Melchizedek's significance is further developed in the New Testament, particularly in the book of Hebrews. In Hebrews 7, the writer explains that Jesus' priesthood is according to the "order of Melchizedek," meaning that it is eternal and superior to the Levitical priesthood. While the Levitical priests offered continual sacrifices for sin, Jesus, like Melchizedek, offers a once-for-all sacrifice that brings eternal redemption (Hebrews 7:27).

The Foreshadowing of a Greater Priesthood

The figures of Adam and Melchizedek both point to the greater reality of priesthood that would be fully revealed in Jesus Christ. Adam's priestly role in the Garden of Eden was compromised by sin, necessitating a new priestly order that could mediate between God and humanity. Melchizedek, as both king and priest, prefigured the perfect union of kingship and priesthood that would be realized in Christ.

In these early glimpses of priesthood, we see the foundations of the biblical concept of a royal priesthood—one in which God's people are called to exercise authority over creation (as Adam did) and to mediate His blessings to the world (as Melchizedek did). The royal priesthood that begins in Genesis finds its fulfillment in the New Testament, where all believers, through Christ, are made "a royal priesthood" (1 Peter 2:9).

As we move forward through the Old Testament, the formalization of the Levitical priesthood under the Mosaic Law provides further insight into the development of priesthood. Yet, as we will see, the limitations of the Levitical system ultimately point forward to the need for a greater High Priest—Jesus, who perfectly combines the roles of king and priest, fulfilling the original purpose of God's people as a kingdom of priests and a holy nation.

In the following sections, we will explore the establishment of the Levitical priesthood in Exodus and Leviticus and how the priestly functions of sacrifice, intercession, and teaching were central to the life of Israel. These elements, while crucial to the old covenant, ultimately point to the perfect and eternal priesthood of Christ under the new covenant.

Exodus: The Nation of Priests

The calling of Israel as a kingdom of priests at Mount Sinai represents one of the most pivotal moments in redemptive history. In Exodus 19:6, God speaks to the people of Israel, declaring, "You shall be to Me a kingdom of priests and a holy nation." This profound statement highlights Israel's unique identity and their role in God's plan of salvation for humanity. Unlike other nations, Israel was called to serve as mediators between God and the world, representing His holiness and revealing His ways to the nations.

The Covenant at Mount Sinai

The backdrop to this momentous declaration is the covenant that God established with Israel at Mount Sinai. After delivering the Israelites from slavery in Egypt, God brought them to this sacred mountain, where He entered into a formal covenant with them. In this covenant, God reaffirmed His relationship with Israel, promising to make them His treasured possession if they obeyed His commands and kept His covenant (Exodus 19:5). In exchange, Israel was called to live according to God's law and to reflect His holiness in every aspect of their lives.

The covenant at Sinai set the stage for Israel's role as a nation of priests. Just as priests in later generations would serve as mediators between God and the people, the entire nation of Israel was now being called to mediate God's presence and blessing to the surrounding nations. Their obedience to the covenant would demonstrate God's character to the world, and their faithfulness would serve as a witness to the other nations about what it meant to be in a relationship with the one true God.

A Kingdom of Priests

When God refers to Israel as a "kingdom of priests," He is highlighting two important aspects of their calling:

1. Royal Authority: Israel, as God's chosen people, was given a royal mandate to govern the land they would inherit, living under the rule of God as their ultimate King. While God would later establish a monarchy with kings such as David, the entire nation was originally envisioned as a "kingdom" in the sense that they were to rule in righteousness under God's authority. Their conduct, their governance, and their way of life were to reflect God's kingship to the world.

2. Priestly Function: The second part of this calling is even more significant. Israel was to be a "nation of priests."

In the ancient world, priests were not only responsible for performing religious duties but also served as mediators between God and the people. They brought the people's offerings to God, interceded on their behalf, and ensured the proper observance of rituals and sacrifices. By calling the entire nation of Israel a kingdom of priests, God was appointing them to a mediatorial role—standing between Him and the rest of the nations. This priestly function meant that Israel was to be a beacon of light, revealing God's holiness, love, and justice to the world.

Israel's Unique Role Among the Nations

This calling positioned Israel in a unique place among the nations of the world. While other nations had their own gods and religious systems, Israel was set apart by their exclusive relationship with the one true God. Their priestly role meant that they were entrusted with the responsibility of making God known to the world through their obedience, worship, and holiness.

Deuteronomy 4:6-8 captures this idea, as Moses tells the Israelites: "Observe them [God's laws] carefully, for this will show your wisdom and understanding to the nations, who will hear about all these decrees and say, 'Surely this great nation is a wise and understanding people.'" Israel's adherence to God's laws was intended to serve as a testimony to the surrounding nations, revealing the character of God and inviting others to know Him.

However, Israel's role as a priestly nation was not just about religious rituals or national identity—it was deeply tied to the mission of God. Israel was meant to be the vehicle through which God's redemptive purposes would be accomplished in the world. From the very beginning, God's plan was to bless all nations through His chosen people, a promise first made to Abraham in Genesis 12:3: "All peoples on earth will be blessed through you."

In this sense, Israel's priestly calling was both a privilege and a responsibility. Their relationship with God was meant to draw the nations to the knowledge of the one true God. As a kingdom of priests, Israel was given the unique task of living as a holy nation, set apart for God's purposes, and acting as a conduit of His grace and truth to the world.

Holiness as a Defining Characteristic

Central to Israel's priestly calling was the concept of holiness. As God said in Exodus 19:6, Israel was to be both "a kingdom of priests" and "a holy nation." Holiness, in biblical terms, refers to being set apart or consecrated for God's purposes. Israel was called to reflect God's holiness in their worship, their laws, their relationships, and their conduct. They were to be distinct from the surrounding nations, living in accordance with God's commands and upholding His standards of righteousness and justice.

This holiness was not just an abstract concept but was woven into the very fabric of Israel's covenant relationship with God. The Levitical laws that God gave to Israel in the books of Exodus, Leviticus, and Deuteronomy were designed to ensure that the people remained ritually pure and morally upright. Every aspect of their lives—from what they ate, to how they worshiped, to how they treated one another—was to reflect God's holiness.

The priesthood of Aaron and the Levites was established within this framework to help maintain the nation's holiness and ensure that Israel remained faithful to their calling. The priests offered sacrifices on behalf of the people, performed rituals of atonement, and instructed the people in the law. In this way, the priestly class played a vital role in helping Israel live up to its identity as a holy nation.

The Tabernacle: A Visible Symbol of Israel's Priestly Role

The construction of the Tabernacle in the wilderness was another important aspect of Israel's priestly calling. The Tabernacle was the physical dwelling place of God's presence among His people, and its design and structure symbolized the holiness of God and the need for mediation between God and humanity.

The Holy of Holies, the innermost sanctuary of the Tabernacle, where the Ark of the Covenant was kept, was the most sacred space in the nation. Only the high priest could enter this space, and only once a year, on the Day of Atonement (Yom Kippur), to make atonement for the sins of the people.

The Tabernacle and later the Temple in Jerusalem became visible symbols of Israel's priestly function. They were reminders that Israel's relationship with God was central to their identity, and that their role as a kingdom of priests was tied to their ability to remain in God's presence and reflect His holiness to the world.

Israel's Successes and Failures in Living as a Priestly Nation

Throughout the Old Testament, Israel's success in living out its priestly calling fluctuated. There were moments when the nation as a whole lived up to its identity as a kingdom of priests, demonstrating God's power and holiness to the surrounding nations. For example, during the reigns of King David and King Solomon, Israel was a beacon of God's blessing and wisdom. The construction of the Temple under

Solomon, along with the nation's prosperity, allowed Israel to fulfill its role as a priestly nation in a visible way.

However, there were also moments of failure. Israel often struggled with idolatry, disobedience, and unfaithfulness to the covenant. The failure of the nation to fully live out its priestly calling led to periods of exile and judgment, as seen in the Babylonian exile. Despite these failures, God remained faithful to His covenant, continuing to call Israel back to Himself through prophets and spiritual leaders.

The Foreshadowing of a New Covenant

Israel's priestly role in the Old Testament points forward to a greater fulfillment in the New Covenant. While Israel was called to be a nation of priests, their inability to fully live up to this calling revealed the need for a perfect mediator—one who could embody both kingship and priesthood in a way that Israel could not. This mediator is found in Jesus Christ, who perfectly fulfills Israel's priestly calling and establishes a new covenant, making a way for all believers to be part of the royal priesthood.

In the New Testament, 1 Peter 2:9 echoes the language of Exodus 19:6, applying it to the church: "But you are a chosen people, a royal priesthood, a holy nation, God's special possession." Through Christ, the church is now called to carry forward Israel's mission, living as a kingdom of priests and reflecting God's holiness to the world.

In the next section, we will explore Leviticus and the formalization of the Levitical priesthood, examining the sacrificial system and the priestly duties that were established to help Israel live as a holy nation. This system, while essential in the old covenant, points forward to the ultimate priestly work of Jesus Christ, who fulfills all of the Old Testament's sacrificial and priestly requirements.

Leviticus: The Function of the Priestly Office

The book of Leviticus provides a detailed account of the responsibilities and rituals associated with the Levitical priesthood, emphasizing the importance of holiness, atonement, and intercession. The Levitical priesthood, established through the line of Aaron, served a critical role in maintaining Israel's covenant relationship with God. However, the sacrificial system and the priestly functions outlined in Leviticus also served as a shadow of the greater and more perfect priesthood that would come through Jesus Christ.

Holiness and Purity

The theme of holiness permeates the entire book of Leviticus. God's holiness is central to Israel's understanding of their relationship with Him, and the priests were charged with upholding this holiness in every aspect of life. In Leviticus 11:45, God declares, "Be holy, for I am holy," making it clear that Israel's calling as a holy nation depended on their adherence to the rituals and practices that God prescribed.

The priesthood, as mediators between God and the people, were responsible for teaching the laws of holiness and ensuring that the people lived in obedience to God's commandments. Priests maintained the sanctity of the tabernacle (and later, the temple), making sure that the people approached God in the proper way, free from impurity and defilement.

The priests themselves were held to the highest standards of holiness. They were required to observe strict rules concerning their own ritual purity, clothing, and behavior. The high priest, in particular, was set apart and was required to wear special garments when ministering before the Lord (Leviticus 8). These garments symbolized the priest's unique role in mediating God's presence and holiness to the people.

Holiness was not just an external requirement but a reflection of the moral and spiritual purity that God demanded of His people. The role of the priest was to help the people maintain this purity, ensuring that their sins were atoned for and that they remained in right standing with God.

The Role of Atonement

One of the primary functions of the Levitical priesthood was to offer atonement for the sins of the people. The system of sacrifices outlined in Leviticus was designed to address both individual and communal sin, restoring the covenant relationship between God and Israel.

The most important day in the Jewish religious calendar was the Day of Atonement (Yom Kippur), described in Leviticus 16. On this day, the high priest entered the Holy of Holies, the innermost chamber of the tabernacle (and later the temple), where the Ark of the Covenant was kept. The high priest was the only one allowed to enter this sacred space, and even he could only enter once a year.

On the Day of Atonement, the high priest offered sacrifices to atone for his own sins as well as the sins of the nation. He sprinkled the blood of a bull and a goat on the mercy seat of the Ark, symbolizing the atonement of Israel's sins through the shedding of blood. The high priest also performed the ritual of the scapegoat, where one goat was sent into the wilderness, symbolically carrying away the sins of the people (Leviticus 16:21-22).

The sacrificial system was based on the principle of substitutionary atonement—the idea that the death of an innocent animal could take the place of the sinner, satisfying God's justice and allowing for the forgiveness of sins. Leviticus 17:11 explains, "For the life of the flesh is in the blood, and I have given it to you upon the altar to make atonement for your souls; for it is the blood that makes atonement for the soul."

However, the sacrificial system was ultimately limited in its effectiveness. While the sacrifices provided temporary atonement, they had to be repeated continually, and they could never fully remove the guilt of sin. The book of Hebrews reflects on the insufficiency of the Levitical sacrifices, stating that "it is impossible for the blood of bulls and goats to take away sins" (Hebrews 10:4). This points to the need for a perfect and once-for-all sacrifice that could fully and permanently atone for sin—a sacrifice that would come through Jesus Christ.

The Role of Intercession

In addition to offering sacrifices, the priests served as intercessors between God and the people. The priestly role of intercession was critical in maintaining the spiritual life of the nation. By offering prayers, sacrifices, and blessings, the priests mediated God's grace and forgiveness to the people.

One of the most well-known examples of priestly intercession is the Aaronic blessing found in Numbers 6:24-26, where Aaron and his descendants were commanded to bless the people of Israel: "The Lord bless you and keep you; the Lord make His face shine on you and be gracious to you; the Lord turn His face toward you and give you peace." This blessing reflected the priestly role of bringing the people into God's favor and ensuring His continued protection and guidance.

The priests also interceded during moments of national crisis. For example, in Numbers 16, during the rebellion of Korah, God's wrath broke out against the people, and a plague began to spread. Aaron, the high priest, took a censer filled with incense and ran into the midst of the congregation, making atonement for the people and stopping the plague (Numbers 16:46-48). This act of intercession highlights the priest's role in standing between God's judgment and the people, pleading for mercy on their behalf.

The Levitical Priesthood as a Shadow of Christ

The entire Levitical priesthood, with its elaborate rituals and sacrifices, served as a shadow of the greater priesthood that would be revealed in Jesus Christ. The limitations of the Levitical system—its temporary sacrifices, imperfect priests, and continual need for atonement—pointed to the need for a perfect high priest and a once-for-all sacrifice.

In the New Testament, the book of Hebrews makes it clear that Jesus is the fulfillment of the Levitical priesthood. Jesus is the perfect high priest who enters the true Holy of Holies—not the earthly tabernacle, but heaven itself—to offer His own blood as a sacrifice for the sins of the world (Hebrews 9:11-12). Unlike the Levitical priests, who had to offer sacrifices continually, Jesus' sacrifice was once and for all, providing eternal redemption for those who believe in Him.

Furthermore, Jesus' priesthood is not based on the Levitical order, but on the order of Melchizedek (Hebrews 7:11-17). As we saw earlier in Genesis, Melchizedek was both a king and a priest, and his priesthood was superior to that of Aaron. Jesus, as the eternal high priest in the order of Melchizedek, perfectly combines the roles of king and priest, bringing together the royal and priestly offices in a way that the Levitical system could only foreshadow.

Jesus' role as high priest is not only superior to the Levitical priesthood, but it also fulfills the deeper spiritual needs that the old covenant could not address. Through His death and resurrection, Jesus opens the way for all believers to enter the presence of God, making them part of a new royal priesthood (1 Peter 2:9). No longer do believers need human priests to mediate between them and God—Jesus Himself is the mediator, and through Him, all believers are made priests unto God.

The Levitical priesthood, with its emphasis on holiness, atonement, and intercession, played a critical role in the spiritual life of Israel. The priests ensured that the people remained in right relationship with God, offering sacrifices and interceding on their behalf. However, the limitations of the Levitical system pointed to the need for a greater and more perfect priesthood, one that would be fulfilled in Jesus Christ.

As we move into the New Testament, we see how Jesus, as the ultimate High Priest, perfectly fulfills and surpasses the Levitical priesthood. His sacrifice brings eternal atonement, and His intercession provides believers with direct access to God. Through Jesus, the royal priesthood is now extended to all who believe, fulfilling the promise of a kingdom of priests and a holy nation that was first given to Israel at Mount Sinai.

In the following chapter, we will explore how the New Covenant fulfills the Old Testament's vision of a royal priesthood, and how believers today are called to live out their identity as kings and priests in the kingdom of God.

CHAPTER 04

JESUS CHRIST – THE ULTIMARE KING AND PRIEST

Jesus as the King of Kings

The kingship of Jesus Christ is one of the most profound themes in the New Testament, affirming His authority over all creation and His ultimate reign as the King of Kings and Lord of Lords. From His royal lineage as the son of David to His heavenly enthronement, Jesus embodies the fulfillment of the Old Testament's promise of a divine king. His kingdom, however, is not bound by the limitations of earthly power; it transcends political borders, earthly thrones, and human understanding. Jesus' kingship is eternal, establishing a reign of justice, peace, and righteousness that will never end.

The Lineage of a King

Jesus' kingship is rooted in His lineage, which traces back to King David, Israel's greatest king. The New Testament begins with the Gospel of Matthew, which opens with a genealogy linking Jesus to David and Abraham, emphasizing His fulfillment of the covenant promises made to both of these patriarchs. Matthew 1:1 declares Jesus as "the son of David, the son of Abraham," immediately connecting Him to the royal line and positioning Him as the heir to David's throne.

This connection to David is significant because of the promises made in the Old Testament that the Messiah would come from David's line and establish an everlasting kingdom. In 2 Samuel 7:12-16, God promises David that his kingdom would endure forever and that one of his descendants would sit on his throne for eternity. This prophecy is known as the Davidic Covenant, and the New Testament writers clearly identify Jesus as the fulfillment of this promise.

Throughout the Gospels, Jesus is repeatedly referred to as the "son of David," particularly in moments when His messianic identity is being recognized. For example, in Matthew 21:9, as Jesus enters Jerusalem, the crowds shout, "Hosanna to the Son of David! Blessed is he who comes in the name of the Lord!" This acknowledgment underscores the expectation that Jesus is the long-awaited King who will bring salvation to Israel and establish God's rule.

The Nature of His Kingdom

While Jesus is clearly identified as the King in the line of David, His kingdom is unlike any earthly kingdom. Jesus' kingship is not characterized by political power, military might, or territorial conquest, as one might expect from a traditional ruler. Instead, His kingdom is spiritual and eternal, transcending earthly limitations and establishing a reign of peace, justice, and righteousness that reflects the very nature of God.

In John 18:36, when questioned by Pontius Pilate about His kingship, Jesus replies, "My kingdom is not of this world. If My kingdom were of this world, My servants would fight, so that I should not be delivered to the Jews; but now My kingdom is not from here." This statement reveals the true nature of Jesus' kingship—it is a divine kingdom, one that operates according to heavenly principles rather than the power structures of the earth.

Jesus' reign is not established through violence or conquest but through His sacrificial love and ultimate victory over sin and death. His enthronement comes not by defeating political enemies but by overcoming the forces of darkness that enslave humanity. The cross, paradoxically, becomes His throne, where He establishes His victory over evil. Through His death and resurrection, Jesus inaugurates His kingdom and makes a way for all who believe in Him to become part of this eternal reign.

The Universal Scope of Jesus' Kingship

While Jesus' kingdom is spiritual, it also has universal implications. Jesus is not just the King of Israel; He is the King of all creation. His authority extends over every nation, tribe, and tongue, and His rule encompasses all things in heaven and on earth. The Gospel of Matthew emphasizes this universal authority in Matthew 28:18, where Jesus declares after His resurrection, "All authority in heaven and on earth has been given to me." This statement asserts Jesus' ultimate kingship over everything, including all powers and principalities.

The book of Revelation further affirms this universal kingship. In Revelation 19:16, Jesus is depicted as the King of Kings and Lord of Lords, riding on a white horse to execute final judgment and establish His eternal rule. This portrayal of Jesus as a conquering king emphasizes His ultimate victory over all forces that oppose God's kingdom. He is not just one king among many; He is the King who reigns supreme over all rulers and authorities, whether spiritual or earthly.

Jesus' kingship is also eternal. Unlike the kings of Israel, whose reigns were temporary and limited by death, Jesus' reign will never end. This eternal kingship fulfills the prophecy made in Isaiah 9:6-7, where the Messiah is described as the "Prince of Peace," whose government and peace will increase without end. The throne of David, which had lain dormant for centuries, is now occupied by Jesus, who reigns forever in perfect righteousness.

Jesus as the Humble King

One of the most striking aspects of Jesus' kingship is His humility. While earthly kings often seek to demonstrate their power through wealth, military strength, and political dominance, Jesus' kingship is marked by humility and servanthood. His royal entry into Jerusalem on a donkey, rather than a war horse, is a clear symbol of this humble kingship (Matthew 21:1-11). The crowds who welcomed Him with palm branches were expecting a political Messiah who would overthrow Roman rule, but Jesus came as the suffering servant, ready to lay down His life for the salvation of humanity.

Jesus' humility is perhaps most powerfully demonstrated in John 13, when He washes the feet of His disciples. This act of service, normally reserved for the lowest of servants, reveals the heart of Jesus' kingship. He came not to be served but to serve, and to give His life as a ransom for many (Mark 10:45). His authority is rooted in His self-giving love, and His rule is characterized by compassion, justice, and mercy.

This humble kingship reaches its climax at the cross. Jesus, the King of the universe, willingly submits to death, taking upon Himself the punishment for sin. In doing so, He defeats the powers of evil and establishes His reign over sin and death. His resurrection three days later is the ultimate confirmation of His kingship, as He triumphs over the grave and ascends to the right hand of the Father, where He reigns eternally.

The Invitation to Share in His Kingdom

As the King of Kings, Jesus invites all who believe in Him to share in His kingdom. Through faith in Christ, believers become co-heirs with Him, participating in His reign and sharing in His royal inheritance. Romans 8:17 declares that "if we are children, then we are heirs—heirs of God and co-heirs with Christ." This incredible reality means that all who are in Christ are not only citizens of His kingdom but are also called to reign with Him.

The New Testament describes believers as kings and priests unto God (Revelation 1:6), a royal priesthood chosen to proclaim the excellencies of God (1 Peter 2:9). This calling reflects the believer's dual identity in Christ: as priests, they serve God and intercede for others; as kings, they exercise spiritual authority, ruling with Christ over sin and darkness.

The ultimate fulfillment of this shared kingship will be realized in the new heavens and the new earth, where believers will reign with Christ forever (Revelation 22:5). In this eternal kingdom, the reign of Jesus will be fully established, and His people will live in perfect harmony with Him, experiencing the fullness of His peace, joy, and righteousness.

In the next section, we will explore how Jesus, as the High Priest, fulfills the priestly role in ways that no earthly priest could, offering the perfect and final sacrifice for sin and interceding eternally on behalf of humanity. Through His unique role as both King and Priest, Jesus embodies the perfect union of authority and mediation, providing the ultimate means of reconciliation between God and humanity.

Jesus as the High Priest

The role of Jesus Christ as the High Priest is one of the most profound aspects of His identity and mission. Unlike the earthly priesthood of the Old Testament, which was limited and temporary, Jesus' priesthood is eternal and perfect. According to the order of Melchizedek, His priesthood surpasses the Levitical priesthood established under the Mosaic Law. In His role as High Priest, Jesus not only intercedes for humanity but also offers Himself as the perfect and final sacrifice for sin, providing a direct way to God and accomplishing what no other priest or sacrifice could.

The Order of Melchizedek

To understand Jesus' priesthood, we must first consider the mysterious figure of Melchizedek, who appears briefly in Genesis 14 as the king of Salem and a priest of the Most High God. Melchizedek blesses Abraham and receives a tithe from him, indicating his superior spiritual authority. This encounter is significant because Melchizedek, as both a king and a priest, foreshadows Jesus' unique dual role as the eternal King and High Priest.

The book of Hebrews elaborates on this connection, explaining that Jesus' priesthood is not like the Levitical priesthood, which was passed down through the line of Aaron, but is according to the order of Melchizedek (Hebrews 7:1-3). This means that Jesus' priesthood is eternal, superior, and not bound by the limitations of the Levitical system. In contrast to the priests of the Old Covenant who served in the earthly tabernacle, Jesus serves in the heavenly sanctuary, offering a perfect and permanent sacrifice.

Hebrews 7:17 quotes Psalm 110:4, which prophetically declares of the Messiah, "You are a priest forever, in the order of Melchizedek." This eternal priesthood, established by divine decree, marks a significant departure from the temporary and flawed system of the Levitical priesthood. Jesus' priesthood is unchangeable and eternal, meaning that He continues to serve as the High Priest forever, providing a continuous means of access to God for believers.

The Superiority of Jesus' Priesthood

The Levitical priesthood, though divinely instituted, was inherently limited. The priests were human, sinful, and subject to death, which meant they had to offer sacrifices for their own sins before they could offer sacrifices for the sins of the people. Moreover, the sacrifices they offered were imperfect and could only provide temporary atonement for sin, requiring continual offerings (Hebrews 10:1-4).

In contrast, Jesus, as the High Priest, is sinless, eternal, and perfect. Unlike the Levitical priests, who had to offer sacrifices repeatedly, Jesus offered Himself as the perfect and final sacrifice, once for all (Hebrews 7:27). His sacrifice was not the blood of animals but His own blood, which is infinitely more valuable and capable of providing complete atonement for the sins of humanity. Hebrews 9:12 declares, "He did not enter by means of the blood of goats and calves;

but He entered the Most Holy Place once for all by His own blood, thus obtaining eternal redemption."

This one-time, all-sufficient sacrifice not only covers sin but completely removes it, reconciling humanity to God in a way that no animal sacrifice ever could. Jesus' priesthood surpasses the Levitical system because He is both the priest and the sacrifice. He willingly laid down His life, offering Himself as the Lamb of God who takes away the sin of the world (John 1:29).

Moreover, Jesus' priesthood is superior because it is based on the power of an indestructible life (Hebrews 7:16). The Levitical priests were subject to death, and their ministry ended when their lives ended. Jesus, however, rose from the dead, and His priesthood continues forever. His resurrection and ascension into heaven mark the beginning of His eternal priestly ministry, where He intercedes for believers at the right hand of God (Hebrews 7:25).

Jesus as the Perfect Sacrifice

One of the most significant aspects of Jesus' high priestly role is that He offers Himself as the perfect sacrifice for sin. In the Old Testament, the priests offered the blood of animals to temporarily atone for the sins of the people. However, these sacrifices were a foreshadowing of the true and perfect sacrifice that would be made through Jesus. As

Hebrews 10:4 explains, "It is impossible for the blood of bulls and goats to take away sins."

Jesus, being sinless, became the perfect Lamb of God, offering His life in place of sinners. His sacrifice was unique in that it was both voluntary and final. Jesus willingly laid down His life for the salvation of humanity, declaring, "I lay down my life for the sheep" (John 10:15). His death on the cross was the ultimate act of love and obedience, fully satisfying the requirements of God's justice.

The book of Hebrews makes it clear that Jesus' sacrifice was a once-for-all offering that brings eternal redemption. Hebrews 9:26 states, "He has appeared once for all at the culmination of the ages to do away with sin by the sacrifice of Himself." This means that Jesus' sacrifice was sufficient to atone for all sins—past, present, and future—and that no further sacrifices are needed. His death accomplished what the Levitical sacrifices could never achieve: the complete removal of sin and the reconciliation of humanity to God.

Through His death and resurrection, Jesus also fulfilled the Day of Atonement rituals described in Leviticus 16. As the High Priest, Jesus entered the Holy of Holies—not the earthly one made by human hands, but the true heavenly sanctuary—and offered His own blood as the ultimate atonement for sin (Hebrews 9:11-12). This act of atonement was not temporary or incomplete, but eternal, bringing peace between God and humanity.

Jesus' Ongoing Intercession

Jesus' priestly work did not end with His death and resurrection. As the High Priest, He continues to intercede for believers, standing as the mediator between God and humanity. Hebrews 7:25 proclaims, "Therefore He is able to save completely those who come to God through Him, because He always lives to intercede for them."

This ongoing intercession means that Jesus, who sits at the right hand of the Father, continually advocates on behalf of His people. His intercession is not just a passive reminder of His sacrifice, but an active, ongoing ministry where He pleads for mercy, grace, and help for believers. This is a source of great comfort and assurance for Christians, knowing that Jesus, as the perfect High Priest, is continually praying for them and providing access to God's throne of grace (Hebrews 4:16).

Because of Jesus' high priestly ministry, believers no longer need a human priest to mediate their relationship with God. Jesus Himself is the mediator of the new covenant, granting believers direct access to God. This is a profound shift from the Old Testament system, where access to God was restricted and mediated through human priests. Now, through Jesus, all believers are able to approach God with confidence, knowing that they are covered by His sacrifice and upheld by His intercession (Hebrews 10:19-22).

A New Way to God

Through His priestly ministry, Jesus has established a new and living way to God (Hebrews 10:20). The old way, marked by the limitations of the Levitical priesthood and the sacrifices of the Old Covenant, has been replaced by the perfect and eternal priesthood of Christ. This new way is not based on human effort, ritual, or sacrifice, but on the finished work of Jesus.

Jesus' priesthood not only provides atonement for sin but also ushers in a new covenant relationship between God and humanity. As the mediator of the new covenant (Hebrews 9:15), Jesus fulfills the promises made in the Old Testament that God would establish a new covenant, one written on the hearts of His people (Jeremiah 31:31-34). Through this covenant, believers are brought into a direct and intimate relationship with God, no longer separated by sin or dependent on human priests for access.

This new way is marked by grace, as believers are no longer bound by the strict regulations of the law but are freely accepted by God through faith in Christ. Jesus' sacrifice is the foundation of this new relationship, and His priesthood guarantees that those who come to Him in faith will be saved, forgiven, and made righteous before God.

Jesus Christ, as the High Priest, surpasses the Levitical priesthood in every way. His priesthood, according to the order of Melchizedek, is eternal, perfect, and unchangeable. By offering Himself as the perfect sacrifice, Jesus has accomplished what no other priest or sacrifice could—He has brought complete and eternal redemption. His ongoing intercession ensures that believers have continual access to God, receiving grace and mercy in their time of need.

Through Jesus, the barrier between God and humanity has been removed, and all who believe in Him are invited to share in His royal priesthood, serving God with confidence and living in the fullness of His grace. As both King and High Priest, Jesus embodies the ultimate fulfillment of God's plan, uniting kingship and priesthood in a way that brings eternal peace, reconciliation, and salvation to all who come to Him.

The Melchizedek Connection

The figure of Melchizedek, as presented in the Old Testament, is one of the most intriguing and significant foreshadowings of Christ's unique priesthood. Melchizedek appears only briefly in Genesis 14:18-20 but plays a crucial role in biblical theology, especially in connection with Jesus' priesthood. His appearance as both a king and a priest foreshadows the dual office of Jesus Christ, and his absence of lineage or recorded death in the scriptures points to the eternal nature of his priesthood. The book of Psalms and, later, the book of Hebrews provide further revelation, showing how Melchizedek's priesthood points to the eternal and superior nature of Christ's priestly office.

Melchizedek in Genesis: The King and Priest of Salem

Melchizedek first appears in Genesis 14 during a significant moment in Abraham's life. After Abraham's victorious battle against the kings who captured his nephew Lot, Melchizedek, described as the king of Salem (likely an ancient reference to Jerusalem) and a priest of God Most High, comes out to meet him. He brings bread and wine, blesses Abraham, and receives a tithe from him (Genesis 14:18-20).

This brief but powerful encounter establishes key aspects of Melchizedek's significance:

1. King of Salem: Melchizedek is both a king and a priest. As the king of Salem, which means "peace," Melchizedek's reign is associated with peace and righteousness. This is a foretaste of Christ, who is the ultimate

King of Peace, bringing reconciliation between God and humanity.

2. Priest of God Most High: Melchizedek is identified as a priest of El Elyon (God Most High), demonstrating that his priesthood is not derived from the Levitical line, which would come much later, but from a higher, universal order. His priesthood is not tied to the laws of Israel but is a priesthood that transcends human history and institutions.

3. Blessing of Abraham: Melchizedek's blessing of Abraham carries great theological weight. In the biblical narrative, the greater blesses the lesser, indicating that Melchizedek holds a position of spiritual superiority over Abraham, the father of the Jewish nation. Abraham's response—giving Melchizedek a tithe—acknowledges this superiority and confirms the significance of Melchizedek's priesthood.

4. Bread and Wine: Melchizedek's offering of bread and wine has been viewed by many Christian theologians as a foreshadowing of the Eucharist, the communion elements that Jesus would later institute. This act points to the sacrificial ministry of Christ, who would offer His own body and blood for the redemption of the world.

The significance of Melchizedek's priesthood becomes clearer in the New Testament, where Jesus is explicitly connected to Melchizedek's order of priesthood, elevating Him above the Levitical priesthood and revealing His eternal nature.

Psalm 110: The Prophetic Connection to Christ

The connection between Melchizedek and the Messiah is further developed in Psalm 110, a psalm that is widely regarded as a Messianic prophecy. In Psalm 110:4, David writes, "The Lord has sworn and will not change His mind: 'You are a priest forever, in the order of Melchizedek.'"

This verse, spoken by God, points directly to the Messiah, who would serve as both King and Priest. It reveals a priesthood that is not based on the temporary, hereditary Levitical system but one that is eternal and divinely appointed. This is significant because it indicates that the coming Messiah's priesthood would be both everlasting and of a higher order than that of Aaron's descendants.

Jesus later identifies Himself as the fulfillment of Psalm 110 in several New Testament passages (Matthew 22:41-46, Mark 12:35-37, Luke 20:41-44), underscoring His divine kingship and eternal priesthood. By being declared a priest forever in the order of Melchizedek, Jesus is shown to fulfill the role of mediator between God and humanity in a way that is both superior and permanent.

Hebrews: The Superior Priesthood of Christ

The book of Hebrews provides the most detailed explanation of the connection between Melchizedek and Christ. Hebrews establishes that Jesus' priesthood, like Melchizedek's, is not based on lineage or human ordination but on divine appointment and eternal existence. The writer of Hebrews argues that Jesus' priesthood surpasses that of the Levitical priests in several key ways:

1. Eternal and Unchanging: In Hebrews 7:3, the writer notes that Melchizedek is "without father or mother, without genealogy, without beginning of days or end of life." While this does not mean that Melchizedek was literally eternal, his lack of recorded genealogy in the biblical text is symbolic of a priesthood that is not bound by human limitations. This prefigures Christ, whose priesthood is eternal. Unlike the Levitical priests who served for a limited time and were replaced by their successors, Jesus, as the eternal Son of God, continues His priestly ministry forever.

2. Superior to the Levitical Priesthood: Hebrews 7:4-10 explains that Melchizedek's priesthood is superior to the Levitical priesthood because Abraham, the forefather of the Levites, gave tithes to Melchizedek and was blessed by him. Since the Levites were still "in the body" of Abraham when this occurred, the writer of Hebrews argues that the Levitical

priesthood is, in a sense, subordinate to the priesthood of Melchizedek—and thus to the priesthood of Christ.

3. Perfect Sacrifice: One of the major weaknesses of the Levitical priesthood was its reliance on repeated sacrifices that could never fully take away sins (Hebrews 10:1-4). In contrast, Jesus, as the ultimate High Priest, offered Himself as the perfect and once-for-all sacrifice (Hebrews 7:27). This makes His priesthood far superior, as it accomplishes what the Levitical system could not—complete and eternal redemption.

4. Permanent Intercession: Hebrews 7:24-25 highlights the fact that Jesus, because He lives forever, has a permanent priesthood. "Therefore He is able to save completely those who come to God through Him, because He always lives to intercede for them." Unlike the Levitical priests, who had to continually offer sacrifices and who themselves died, Jesus' priesthood is everlasting, and He continually intercedes for believers. This ongoing intercession means that believers have continual access to God through Christ, and their salvation is secure because Jesus is always acting on their behalf.

5. A New Covenant: Jesus' priesthood, in the order of Melchizedek, also brings with it a new covenant. In Hebrews 8, the writer explains that Jesus' priestly ministry is founded

on better promises than the old covenant, which was limited and dependent on human obedience to the law. Through Jesus' priesthood, the new covenant is established, which is based on God's grace and the perfect sacrifice of Christ. This new covenant promises the forgiveness of sins and the transformation of hearts, fulfilling the prophecy of Jeremiah 31:31-34.

The Eternal Nature of Christ's Priesthood

The Melchizedek connection reveals not only the superiority of Jesus' priesthood but also its eternal nature. Jesus is a priest forever, and His ministry is ongoing. This eternal priesthood means that believers are never without an advocate before the throne of God. Unlike the temporary priesthoods of the Old Testament, which could be interrupted by death or sin, Jesus' priesthood is unbreakable, eternal, and perfect.

His eternal priesthood offers believers both security and confidence. Because He is always interceding, they can approach God's throne of grace boldly, knowing that their High Priest has already secured their access through His blood (Hebrews 4:16). Jesus' intercession is not merely symbolic; it is an active and continuous work, ensuring that the redemption He achieved on the cross is applied to believers for all time.

The figure of Melchizedek serves as a profound type, pointing to the unique and eternal priesthood of Jesus Christ. His appearance in Genesis and his role in Psalm 110 foreshadow the superior, divine, and eternal nature of the Messiah's priesthood, which is fully revealed in the book of Hebrews. Jesus, as a priest in the order of Melchizedek, surpasses the limitations of the Levitical system, offering a perfect sacrifice, establishing a new covenant, and providing eternal intercession for believers.

Through His priesthood, Jesus brings eternal salvation, giving believers direct access to God and the assurance that their High Priest lives forever to intercede on their behalf. This connection between Melchizedek and Christ highlights the profound depth of God's redemptive plan, fulfilled perfectly in the person of Jesus, who is both the King of Kings and the High Priest of an eternal, unshakable kingdom.

CHAPTER 05

THE NEW COVENANT AND THE BELIEVER'S ROLE

The Fulfillment of Prophecies

The New Covenant, inaugurated by the death and resurrection of Jesus Christ, stands as the fulfillment of numerous Old Testament prophecies, ushering in a new era in God's relationship with humanity. Unlike the Old Covenant, which was based on the law given through Moses, the New Covenant is characterized by grace, a personal relationship with God, and the indwelling of the Holy Spirit. Through Christ's sacrificial death, this covenant establishes believers as partakers in the royal priesthood, calling them to live as holy representatives of God in the world. The New Covenant fulfills ancient promises made to Israel and extends them to all who place their faith in Christ, Jew and Gentile alike.

The Prophetic Background of the New Covenant

The concept of the New Covenant is rooted in the prophetic promises of the Old Testament. God's people had long struggled to keep the Old Covenant, which required obedience to the law. This covenant, though holy and just, revealed the weakness of human nature, as Israel continually fell into disobedience, idolatry, and spiritual rebellion. The failure of the Old Covenant system pointed to the need for something greater—a new way in which God's people could be empowered to live in righteousness and fellowship with Him.

The prophet Jeremiah was the first to explicitly prophesy about the coming New Covenant. In Jeremiah 31:31-34, God promises:

> "The days are coming," declares the Lord, "when I will make a new covenant with the people of Israel and with the people of Judah. It will not be like the covenant I made with their ancestors when I took them by the hand to lead them out of Egypt, because they broke my covenant, though I was a husband to them," declares the Lord. "This is the covenant I will make with the people of Israel after that time," declares the Lord. "I will put my law in their minds and write it on their hearts. I will be their God, and they will be my people."

This prophecy highlights several key features of the New Covenant:

1. A Transformative Relationship: Unlike the Old Covenant, which was external and centered around written laws, the New Covenant would involve the transformation of the heart. God's law would be internalized, written on the hearts and minds of His people, enabling them to live in obedience out of love rather than mere obligation.

2. Intimacy with God: The New Covenant promises a more intimate relationship between God and His people. "I will be their God, and they will be my people" echoes the covenantal language used throughout the Old Testament, but under the New Covenant, this relationship is deepened through the work of the Holy Spirit.

3. Forgiveness of Sins: Jeremiah's prophecy also includes the assurance of forgiveness: "For I will forgive their wickedness and will remember their sins no more" (Jeremiah 31:34). This forgiveness would come through the sacrificial death of Christ, which would fully atone for sin, something that the sacrifices of the Old Covenant could never achieve.

Another key prophecy concerning the New Covenant is found in Ezekiel 36:26-27, where God promises to give His people a "new heart" and put His Spirit within them, empowering them to walk in His ways. This prophecy anticipates the indwelling of the Holy Spirit, a central feature of the New Covenant, which enables believers to live out their priestly calling.

The Inauguration of the New Covenant

The New Covenant was inaugurated through the death and resurrection of Jesus Christ. At the Last Supper, Jesus explicitly identified His impending death as the moment when the New Covenant would be established. As He shared the cup with His disciples, He said, "This cup is the new covenant in my blood, which is poured out for you" (Luke 22:20). Jesus' blood, shed on the cross, sealed the New Covenant, just as the blood of sacrifices had sealed the Old Covenant at Mount Sinai (Exodus 24:8).

However, the New Covenant goes far beyond the Old Covenant in its scope and effect. Through His death, Jesus offered a perfect and final sacrifice for sin, bringing about complete atonement and reconciliation between God and humanity. This sacrifice did what the blood of bulls and goats could never do—it provided eternal redemption (Hebrews 9:12). With the Old Covenant, the people were bound to the law, and their relationship with God was mediated through priests. Under the New Covenant, however, Jesus serves as the final High Priest and the perfect mediator (Hebrews 9:15), granting believers direct access to God.

Through Jesus' resurrection, the power of the New Covenant was fully realized. His victory over sin and death opened the way for all who believe to receive eternal life and enter into a new, unbreakable relationship with God. The New Covenant, then, is not just a reformation of the old system but a completely new and transformative reality, one that fulfills the promises made to Israel while extending the blessings of salvation to the entire world.

The Indwelling of the Holy Spirit

A defining feature of the New Covenant is the indwelling of the Holy Spirit. As prophesied by Ezekiel and fulfilled at Pentecost (Acts 2), the Holy Spirit is now given to all believers as a seal and guarantee of their inheritance in Christ. The Holy Spirit is the agent of transformation, writing God's laws on the hearts of His people and empowering them to live in holiness.

Under the Old Covenant, the law was external, written on stone tablets and dependent on human effort to obey. But in the New Covenant, the Holy Spirit works within believers, transforming their hearts and minds so that they desire to follow God's commands. Romans 8:9-11 explains that those who belong to Christ have the Spirit of God dwelling in them, giving them life and enabling them to walk in the Spirit rather than in the flesh.

The indwelling of the Holy Spirit also empowers believers to fulfill their role as part of the royal priesthood. Through the Spirit, believers are able to offer spiritual sacrifices to God (1 Peter 2:5) and intercede for others. The Spirit equips them with spiritual gifts (1 Corinthians 12) to serve the church and advance God's kingdom. This is a radical shift from the Old Covenant, where only a select group of priests could serve in the temple. Under the New Covenant, all believers, through the indwelling of the Spirit, are priests with direct access to God and the ability to minister to others.

Believers as Partakers in the Royal Priesthood

One of the greatest privileges of the New Covenant is that it establishes all believers as part of a royal priesthood, a calling that was once limited to Israel and the Levitical priesthood. 1 Peter 2:9 declares, "But you are a chosen people, a royal priesthood, a holy nation, God's special possession, that you may declare the praises of Him who called you out of darkness into His wonderful light." This verse emphasizes the continuity of God's plan from the Old Covenant to the New, where believers in Christ now inherit the priestly role once assigned to Israel.

As members of this royal priesthood, believers are called to:

1. Declare God's Praises: The primary role of priests is to worship and glorify God. Under the New Covenant, believers are called to proclaim the goodness and greatness of God, sharing the gospel of Christ and bearing witness to His saving power.

2. Offer Spiritual Sacrifices: While the Old Covenant priesthood was centered on animal sacrifices, the New Covenant priesthood involves offering "spiritual sacrifices" acceptable to God (1 Peter 2:5). These sacrifices include worship, prayer, acts of service, and living lives of obedience to God's Word (Romans 12:1). The sacrifices believers offer are no longer about atoning for sin—that was accomplished by Christ—but about living out a life of devotion and gratitude.

3. Intercede for Others: As priests, believers are also called to intercede on behalf of others. This includes praying for those who are lost, offering support and encouragement to fellow believers, and standing in the gap for those in need. Through prayer and spiritual authority, believers participate in God's work of bringing others into His kingdom.

4. Live in Holiness: Just as the Old Testament priests were called to be holy, so too are believers under the New Covenant. Holiness is a defining characteristic of the royal

priesthood, as believers are set apart for God's service and called to reflect His character in every aspect of their lives.

A Personal Relationship with God

The New Covenant is ultimately characterized by a deep and personal relationship with God. Unlike the Old Covenant, where access to God was mediated through priests and rituals, the New Covenant allows every believer to come directly to God through Jesus Christ. This personal relationship is marked by intimacy, love, and communion with God.

In Hebrews 4:16, believers are invited to "approach God's throne of grace with confidence, so that we may receive mercy and find grace to help us in our time of need." This bold access to God is one of the great privileges of the New Covenant. Through Christ, believers can enter the presence of God without fear, knowing that they are fully accepted and forgiven.

Moreover, the Holy Spirit dwelling within each believer enables ongoing fellowship with God. The Spirit testifies to believers that they are God's children (Romans 8:16) and continually works to conform them to the image of Christ. This personal relationship is the essence of the New

Covenant—a relationship not based on external laws but on an internal transformation through the Spirit of God.

The New Covenant, established by the death and resurrection of Jesus Christ, is the fulfillment of Old Testament prophecies and the culmination of God's redemptive plan. It brings forgiveness of sins, the indwelling of the Holy Spirit, and a new, transformative relationship with God. Through this covenant, believers are made part of a royal priesthood, called to worship God, offer spiritual sacrifices, and intercede for others. This new identity empowers believers to live as holy representatives of God in the world, sharing in the blessings of the New Covenant and proclaiming the gospel of Christ.

In the next chapter, we will explore how believers can live out their calling as kings and priests in the everyday realities of life, walking in spiritual authority and serving others with the heart of Christ.

The Believer's Authority as Kings

Through the New Covenant, believers are not only called to be part of a royal priesthood but are also granted authority to reign in life as kings through their union with Jesus Christ, the King of Kings. This authority is rooted in Christ's victory over sin, death, and all the powers of darkness. Believers are empowered to exercise spiritual dominion, overcome evil, and steward God's creation with wisdom and integrity. This kingship is not about worldly power or dominance but about living in the authority of Christ, bringing His kingdom to bear on every area of life.

Reigning in Life through Christ

The foundation for the believer's kingship is found in Romans 5:17, which says, "For if, by the trespass of the one man, death reigned through that one man, how much more will those who receive God's abundant provision of grace and of the gift of righteousness reign in life through the one man, Jesus Christ!" This verse emphasizes that through Christ, believers are no longer under the dominion of sin and death but are empowered to reign in life.

This kingship is not a position that believers achieve through their own merit or effort, but rather it is a gift of grace. Through faith in Jesus, believers receive the righteousness of Christ, which restores them to a position of authority that was lost through Adam's sin. Just as Adam was given dominion over creation but lost it through disobedience, Christ restores that dominion to all who belong to Him.

To reign in life means that believers are called to live in victory over the forces that once enslaved them—sin, fear, death, and the devil. It means that they are no longer subject to the tyranny of sin or the oppressive influences of the world but are empowered by the Holy Spirit to live in freedom and authority.

Exercising Spiritual Dominion

As kings, believers are called to exercise spiritual dominion over the forces of evil. This dominion is rooted in the authority of Christ, who declared after His resurrection, "All authority in heaven and on earth has been given to me" (Matthew 28:18). Believers, being united with Christ, share in this authority and are commissioned to advance His kingdom by combating the spiritual forces of darkness.

In Ephesians 6:10-18, Paul reminds believers that their battle is not against flesh and blood but against "the rulers, the authorities, the powers of this dark world and against the spiritual forces of evil in the heavenly realms." As kings in Christ's kingdom, believers are equipped with spiritual armor—the belt of truth, the breastplate of righteousness, the shield of faith, the helmet of salvation, the sword of the Spirit, and the gospel of peace. With this armor, they are able to stand firm against the schemes of the devil and claim victory over spiritual opposition.

This spiritual dominion also involves the authority to cast out demons, heal the sick, and break the power of sin in their lives and in the lives of others. Jesus promised His disciples, "I have given you authority to trample on snakes and scorpions and to overcome all the power of the enemy; nothing will harm you" (Luke 10:19). This authority extends to every believer, empowering them to confront evil and to bring healing and restoration in the name of Jesus.

Spiritual dominion, however, is not about self-exaltation or personal power; it is about advancing God's kingdom and bringing others into the freedom and life that Christ offers. Believers exercise this authority humbly, recognizing that it is Christ's power working through them, not their own.

Stewarding Creation with Wisdom and Integrity

The kingship of believers also involves stewarding God's creation with wisdom, integrity, and responsibility. When God created humanity, He gave them dominion over the earth, commanding them to "fill the earth and subdue it" and to "rule over" all living creatures (Genesis 1:28). This mandate to rule was never meant to be an abusive or exploitative authority but a stewardship—a responsibility to care for and cultivate creation in a way that reflects God's character and purposes.

Through the New Covenant, believers are restored to their original calling as stewards of God's creation. This stewardship involves caring for the environment, using resources wisely, and cultivating the earth in ways that honor

God and benefit others. It is a reflection of God's own care for His creation, and it involves taking responsibility for the world around us, ensuring that it thrives under our watch.

Believers are also called to steward not just the physical creation but every aspect of their lives—time, talents, relationships, finances, and opportunities. As kings, they are entrusted with the responsibility to make decisions that reflect God's will and bring about His purposes on earth. This requires wisdom, discernment, and integrity, all of which are provided through the guidance of the Holy Spirit.

In Matthew 25:14-30, Jesus tells the parable of the talents, where a master entrusts his servants with money and expects them to invest it wisely. The faithful servants are rewarded for their stewardship, while the unfaithful servant is rebuked for failing to use what was entrusted to him. This parable illustrates the principle that believers, as kings under Christ, are called to wisely manage what God has given them—whether it be spiritual gifts, material resources, or opportunities for influence.

Combating Evil with Righteousness

Another key aspect of the believer's kingship is the responsibility to combat evil with righteousness, both in their personal lives and in the world around them. The authority given to believers is not just to resist personal temptation but to stand against the systems of injustice, corruption, and evil that exist in the world.

In Romans 12:21, Paul instructs believers, "Do not be overcome by evil, but overcome evil with good." This means that believers are called to actively bring the light of Christ into the darkest places, challenging systems of oppression, standing up for the marginalized, and promoting justice and righteousness in their communities. Jesus' kingship is one of justice and peace, and believers, as His representatives, are called to reflect those values in their own spheres of influence.

This may involve speaking out against injustice, supporting causes that promote human dignity, and working to transform society according to the values of God's kingdom. Whether it's in business, education, politics, or everyday relationships, believers are called to bring the righteousness of God into every area of life.

Living with Integrity and Purpose

As kings under Christ, believers are also called to live with integrity and a sense of purpose. Kingship involves not only exercising authority but doing so in a way that reflects the character of Christ. In the Old Testament, kings were often judged by their faithfulness to God and their ability to lead the people in righteousness. In the same way, believers are called to live lives of moral integrity, seeking to honor God in everything they do.

This involves making decisions based on God's truth rather than worldly values, maintaining honesty in all dealings, and being faithful to the responsibilities that God has entrusted to them. As Proverbs 11:3 states, "The integrity of the upright guides them, but the unfaithful are destroyed by their duplicity." Integrity is essential to fulfilling the role of kingship, as it ensures that the authority given to believers is used for God's purposes rather than personal gain.

Believers are also called to live with a sense of purpose, understanding that their kingship is part of God's larger plan for the world. They are not kings in isolation but are part of a royal priesthood that is working to advance God's kingdom on earth. This means that every decision, every action, and every word has eternal significance. Living with this sense of purpose brings meaning to even the mundane tasks of life, as believers understand that they are serving Christ and bringing His kingdom to bear on the world around them.

Believers are granted the authority to reign in life through Christ, reflecting the kingship that Jesus has bestowed upon them through the New Covenant. This kingship is not about earthly power or dominance but is rooted in spiritual authority, allowing believers to exercise dominion over sin and evil, steward God's creation, and live lives of integrity and purpose. As kings, believers are called to combat evil with righteousness, promote justice, and live in a way that reflects the character of Christ.

This kingship is both a gift and a responsibility. It is a calling to live in the fullness of the authority that Christ has given, bringing His kingdom to earth in every sphere of life. As believers embrace their role as kings, they are empowered to reign with Christ, advancing His kingdom and glorifying God in all they do.

In the next chapter, we will explore the believer's responsibility as priests, focusing on the call to intercede, offer spiritual sacrifices, and live lives of holiness before God and others.

The Believer's Responsibility as Priests

In addition to their role as kings, believers in Christ are also called to the responsibility of priests. This dual role of kingship and priesthood is central to the New Covenant, as believers are described in 1 Peter 2:9 as "a chosen people, a royal priesthood, a holy nation, God's special possession." As priests, believers are set apart for a life of holiness, intercession, and service, offering spiritual sacrifices to God and representing His presence to the world. This priestly role is not confined to a select group but is the calling of every Christian, making the whole church a community of priests unto God.

The Call to Holiness

The foundational responsibility of the priesthood is the call to holiness. In the Old Testament, priests were required to live lives of ritual and moral purity, maintaining a standard of holiness as they served in the temple and mediated between God and the people. Under the New Covenant, all believers are called to this same standard of holiness, not through ritual purity but through the sanctifying work of the Holy Spirit.

1 Peter 1:15-16 echoes God's call to Israel in the Old Testament: "But just as He who called you is holy, so be holy in all you do; for it is written: 'Be holy, because I am holy.'" Holiness, for the believer, means being set apart for God's purposes, living in a way that reflects His character. This holiness is not something achieved through human effort alone but is the result of the transformative power of Christ's sacrifice and the Holy Spirit's work in the believer's life.

Living as holy priests means that believers are to reflect God's purity, love, and righteousness in every area of their lives. They are called to live differently from the world, avoiding sin and embracing God's ways. Romans 12:1 captures this priestly call to holiness: "Therefore, I urge you, brothers and sisters, in view of God's mercy, to offer your bodies as a living sacrifice, holy and pleasing to God—this is your true and proper worship." As priests, believers offer themselves as living sacrifices, dedicating their whole lives to God's service.

This holiness is not merely for personal piety; it is also a witness to the world. As believers live in holiness, they reveal God's character to others and draw them toward Him. The priestly call to holiness is therefore both an individual and corporate responsibility, as the church reflects the holiness of God to the world.

The Ministry of Intercession

One of the key functions of the priesthood in the Old Testament was the role of intercession—praying and standing in the gap on behalf of the people before God. The high priest, in particular, would enter the Holy of Holies once a year on the Day of Atonement to intercede for the nation of Israel, offering sacrifices for their sins. Under the New Covenant, Jesus, as the ultimate High Priest, has made the final and perfect atonement for sin through His sacrifice. However, the responsibility of intercession now extends to all believers, who are called to pray and intercede for others.

1 Timothy 2:1 urges believers to engage in intercession: "I urge, then, first of all, that petitions, prayers, intercession and thanksgiving be made for all people." As priests, believers are called to pray for those who are in need, whether they be fellow believers, leaders, or those who are lost. This ministry of intercession is one of the most powerful ways in which believers participate in God's work of redemption, standing before God on behalf of others and asking for His mercy, grace, and intervention.

Believers' intercession is modeled on Christ's own intercessory work. Hebrews 7:25 declares that Christ "always lives to intercede" for believers, and through Him, believers are empowered to intercede for the needs of others. This intercessory prayer is an essential part of the priestly role, as it brings the concerns, struggles, and needs of others before God's throne of grace.

Intercession is not limited to prayer for physical needs but also includes spiritual warfare and praying for the advancement of God's kingdom. Ephesians 6:18 instructs believers to "pray in the Spirit on all occasions with all kinds of prayers and requests," highlighting the breadth of the priestly ministry of intercession. Whether it is praying for the salvation of others, for healing, for wisdom, or for justice, intercession is a priestly act that aligns the believer with God's heart and purposes for the world.

Presenting Spiritual Sacrifices

Under the Old Covenant, priests offered animal sacrifices as atonement for sin and as acts of worship. However, the sacrifices of the Old Testament were limited and could never fully take away sin (Hebrews 10:4). With the coming of Christ, the sacrificial system of the Old Covenant was fulfilled, and the need for animal sacrifices was done away with. Nevertheless, believers, as priests under the New Covenant, are still called to offer spiritual sacrifices to God.

1 Peter 2:5 explains, "You also, like living stones, are being built into a spiritual house to be a holy priesthood, offering spiritual sacrifices acceptable to God through Jesus Christ." These spiritual sacrifices include acts of worship, prayer, praise, thanksgiving, and service. While no longer required to offer sacrifices for atonement, believers present their lives as offerings to God, continually giving of themselves in worship and service.

Some examples of these spiritual sacrifices include:

1. Prayer and Praise: Prayer is a spiritual sacrifice that reflects the priestly duty of offering incense before God, as seen in Revelation 5:8, where the prayers of the saints are depicted as incense before the throne of God. Similarly,

Hebrews 13:15 calls believers to "continually offer to God a sacrifice of praise—the fruit of lips that openly profess His name." Praising God in worship is an act of spiritual sacrifice that acknowledges His goodness and sovereignty.

2. Acts of Love and Service: Believers also offer spiritual sacrifices through their acts of love and service to others. Hebrews 13:16 says, "And do not forget to do good and to share with others, for with such sacrifices God is pleased." As priests, believers are called to serve one another in love, reflecting the servant-heartedness of Christ. Whether it is through generosity, compassion, or acts of kindness, these acts of love are sacrifices that honor God.

3. Living a Holy Life: As already mentioned, living a life of holiness is itself a spiritual sacrifice. By choosing to live according to God's ways rather than the world's, believers offer their lives as a pleasing sacrifice to God. This daily commitment to holiness, purity, and righteousness is a reflection of the believer's role as a priest, dedicated to God's service.

4. Offering Our Gifts and Talents: The spiritual gifts that believers are given by the Holy Spirit are also to be used as spiritual sacrifices in the service of God. Romans 12:6-8 encourages believers to use their gifts—whether it be teaching, serving, encouraging, or leading—for the building

up of the church and the advancement of God's kingdom. When believers use their gifts for God's glory, they are offering their talents as spiritual sacrifices that contribute to the work of the priesthood.

The Call to Serve

As priests, believers are also called to serve both God and others. In the Old Testament, priests were dedicated to serving in the tabernacle or temple, performing rituals, offering sacrifices, and ensuring that the people remained in right relationship with God. Under the New Covenant, the priestly service of believers extends to every area of life.

Believers serve God by worshiping Him, obeying His commands, and advancing His kingdom through their words and actions. This service is not confined to formal religious settings but encompasses every aspect of life. Colossians 3:23-24 reminds believers, "Whatever you do, work at it with all your heart, as working for the Lord, not for human masters." Whether at work, at home, or in ministry, believers are called to serve God with excellence and dedication, recognizing that their entire lives are an offering to Him.

In addition to serving God, believers are called to serve others. Jesus modeled this servant leadership when He washed the feet of His disciples, teaching them that "whoever wants to become great among you must be your servant"

(Mark 10:43). As priests, believers are called to humble service, putting the needs of others before their own and reflecting Christ's love through their actions.

This call to service is at the heart of the priestly role. Whether it's serving within the church, caring for the poor, or ministering to those in need, believers are called to represent Christ's love and compassion to the world. Service is a tangible expression of the believer's priestly responsibility, demonstrating the heart of God to those who may not yet know Him.

As priests in the New Covenant, believers are called to live lives marked by holiness, intercession, and service. They offer spiritual sacrifices to God, present prayers and praises as offerings, and dedicate their lives to serving both God and others. This priestly calling is not reserved for a select few but is the responsibility of every believer, who is empowered by the Holy Spirit to live out this sacred role.

Through their priestly work, believers participate in God's ongoing redemptive mission, bringing His presence into the world and standing

in the gap for others. This calling to be both kings and priests is a powerful reminder that the Christian life is one of both authority and service, as believers reign with Christ while also serving as His representatives on earth.

CHAPTER 06

LIVING AS KINGS AND PRIESTS TODAY

Spiritual Authority and Dominion

In the New Covenant, believers are called to live out their dual identity as kings and priests—a profound calling that reflects the authority and responsibility given to them by Christ. As kings, believers are entrusted with spiritual authority and dominion, enabling them to reign in life through Christ, to overcome sin, and to stand against the powers of darkness. Living as kings today involves recognizing the authority granted by Jesus and actively participating in the advancement of God's kingdom on earth. This chapter explores what it means to live in spiritual authority and how believers can exercise this dominion in their daily lives.

Recognizing Spiritual Authority

The foundation of the believer's kingship is the recognition of their spiritual authority in Christ Jesus. When Jesus rose from the dead, He declared, "All authority in heaven and on earth has been given to me" (Matthew 28:18). Through His victory over sin, death, and Satan, Jesus reclaimed the dominion that was lost in the Garden of Eden, and He now shares that authority with His followers.

Believers are not passive participants in this authority—they are active partakers. Ephesians 2:6 explains that believers are seated with Christ "in the heavenly realms," a position of authority and dominion. This spiritual authority is not based on personal merit or effort but is rooted in the finished work of Christ. As believers, we stand in the authority of the risen Christ, empowered by the Holy Spirit to live victoriously over sin and to expand God's kingdom.

Understanding and accepting this spiritual authority is the first step in living as kings today. Many believers struggle with feelings of inadequacy or powerlessness, not realizing that Christ has already given them the authority to overcome these struggles. Luke 10:19 reassures believers of this authority: "I have given you authority to trample on snakes and scorpions and to overcome all the power of the enemy; nothing will harm you."

Living in this authority requires faith—faith that what Christ accomplished on the cross is enough and that believers are equipped to walk in victory. It involves rejecting the lies of the enemy and embracing the truth that believers are no longer slaves to sin, fear, or the powers of darkness. In Romans 8:37, Paul declares that believers are "more than conquerors through Him who loved us," affirming the victorious identity of the believer in Christ.

Overcoming Sin and Living in Victory

One of the primary expressions of spiritual kingship is the victory over sin. Before Christ, humanity was enslaved to sin, unable to break free from its power. However, through Christ's death and resurrection, sin's hold has been broken, and believers are no longer under its dominion. Romans 6:14 affirms this truth: "For sin shall no longer be your master, because you are not under the law, but under grace."

Living as a king involves recognizing that, through Christ, believers have been set free from the power of sin. This means that sin no longer has the final say in a believer's life. While temptations and struggles will still arise, believers are no longer powerless in the face of sin. They have been given the authority to resist temptation, to overcome sinful habits, and to live in the righteousness of Christ.

This victory is not achieved through willpower or self-discipline alone but through the grace of God and the empowerment of the Holy Spirit. Galatians 5:16 instructs believers to "walk by the Spirit, and you will not gratify the desires of the flesh." The Spirit empowers believers to live according to God's ways, giving them the strength to say no to sin and to pursue holiness.

Victory over sin also includes overcoming guilt, shame, and condemnation. Satan often tries to accuse and discourage believers by reminding them of their past failures. However, Romans 8:1 declares, "There is now no condemnation for those who are in Christ Jesus." As kings, believers must stand firm in the truth of their forgiveness and freedom, rejecting the accusations of the enemy and embracing their identity as beloved children of God.

Standing Against the Powers of Darkness

In addition to overcoming sin, living as kings also involves standing against the powers of darkness. Spiritual warfare is a reality for every believer, and part of exercising spiritual authority is recognizing and resisting the strategies of the enemy. Ephesians 6:12 reminds believers that "our struggle is not against flesh and blood, but against the rulers, against the authorities, against the powers of this dark world and against the spiritual forces of evil in the heavenly realms."

Jesus has already defeated Satan and his kingdom of darkness through His death and resurrection. However, the enemy continues to wage war against believers, seeking to deceive, distract, and destroy. As kings, believers are called to stand firm in the authority of Christ, resisting the devil and advancing God's kingdom in the world.

James 4:7 provides a simple but powerful instruction: "Submit yourselves, then, to God. Resist the devil, and he will flee from you." By submitting to God and standing firm in faith, believers can resist the attacks of the enemy and see him flee. This resistance involves both prayer and action—prayer to align with God's will and seek His protection, and action to walk in obedience to God's Word.

The armor of God, described in Ephesians 6:13-17, is essential for standing against the powers of darkness. Believers are instructed to "put on the full armor of God," which includes the belt of truth, the breastplate of righteousness, the shield of faith, the helmet of salvation, and the sword of the Spirit. This armor equips believers to stand firm in the face of spiritual opposition, confident that Christ's victory is their victory.

Part of standing against darkness also involves advancing God's kingdom. Jesus commissioned His disciples to "go and make disciples of all nations" (Matthew 28:19), a command that extends to all believers. As kings, believers are called to actively participate in bringing the light of Christ into a world darkened by sin, injustice, and evil. This includes sharing the gospel, praying for the lost, and working for justice and righteousness in their communities.

Advancing God's Kingdom on Earth

Living as kings also means participating in the advancement of God's kingdom on earth. Jesus taught His disciples to pray, "Your kingdom come, Your will be done, on earth as it is in heaven" (Matthew 6:10). This prayer reflects the mission of every believer: to see God's kingdom established in every sphere of life.

God's kingdom is not about political power or earthly wealth; it is about righteousness, peace, and joy in the Holy Spirit (Romans 14:17). As kings, believers are called to live out these kingdom values in their families, workplaces, churches, and communities. This involves promoting justice, showing mercy, and living in a way that reflects the character of Christ.

One of the primary ways believers advance God's kingdom is through servant leadership. Jesus, the ultimate King, demonstrated this by washing His disciples' feet and laying down His life for others. In the same way, believers are called to lead by serving, using their authority not for personal gain but to bless and uplift others.

Matthew 20:25-28 provides a clear contrast between worldly leadership and kingdom leadership. Jesus told His disciples, "You know that the rulers of the Gentiles lord it over them, and their high officials exercise authority over them. Not so with you. Instead, whoever wants to become great among you must be your servant." Living as a king in God's kingdom means serving others, advancing God's will, and promoting His love and justice in all that we do.

Believers also advance God's kingdom by living out the gospel in their everyday lives. This includes sharing the good news of Jesus with others, but it also means embodying the principles of the kingdom—love, humility, forgiveness, and generosity. By living out these values, believers bring a foretaste of God's coming kingdom into the present world, pointing others to the reign of Christ.

Living with Purpose and Responsibility

As kings under Christ, believers are entrusted with great responsibility. This responsibility includes not only spiritual authority but also stewardship of the resources, gifts, and opportunities that God has given them. In the parable of the talents (Matthew 25:14-30), Jesus teaches that His followers will be held accountable for how they use the gifts and resources He has entrusted to them. Faithfulness in these responsibilities is a hallmark of living as a king.

Believers are called to live with purpose, understanding that their authority and influence are not meant for self-serving ends but for the glory of God and the advancement of His kingdom. Whether in their personal lives, careers, or ministries, believers are called to exercise their kingship with wisdom, integrity, and humility, always seeking to align their actions with God's will.

Living as kings today means embracing the spiritual authority given by Christ and walking in victory over sin, standing firm against the powers of darkness, and advancing God's kingdom on earth. Believers are called to recognize the authority that Christ has already given them, to live in the freedom and victory of that authority, and to use it to promote justice, peace, and righteousness in their communities.

This kingship is not about worldly power or personal gain but about advancing the mission of God in the world—bringing His love, truth, and grace to those in need. As kings under the reign of Christ, believers are called to live with purpose, exercising their authority with humility and integrity, and partnering with God in the ongoing work of redemption.

In the next section, we will further explore how believers can live as priests, walking in holiness, offering spiritual sacrifices, and interceding on behalf of others. Together, the roles of kings and priests empower believers to fulfill their divine calling in Christ and bring God's kingdom to earth.

Intercession and Mediation

One of the most significant roles of the believer's priesthood is that of intercession and mediation. As priests under the New Covenant, believers are called to stand in the gap for others, bringing their needs, struggles, and requests before God in prayer. This priestly ministry goes beyond personal prayers to encompass a broader responsibility of proclaiming the gospel and leading others to reconciliation with God. Through intercession and mediation, believers participate in God's redemptive work, serving as a bridge between God and humanity, just as Christ intercedes on behalf of all believers.

The Call to Intercede for Others

Intercession is a central aspect of the believer's priestly duty. In the Old Testament, priests would intercede for the people of Israel, offering sacrifices and prayers on their behalf. The high priest, in particular, would enter the Holy of Holies once a year on the Day of Atonement to make atonement for the sins of the nation (Leviticus 16). This role of intercession was vital in maintaining the covenant relationship between God and His people.

Under the New Covenant, all believers are called to this ministry of intercession. 1 Timothy 2:1 urges believers: "I urge, then, first of all, that petitions, prayers, intercession and thanksgiving be made for all people." Intercession is the act of standing in the gap, praying on behalf of others, and bringing their needs before God. As priests, believers are not only responsible for their own spiritual growth but are also called to pray for the well-being and salvation of others.

This ministry of intercession is modeled on Christ's own work. Hebrews 7:25 explains that Jesus "always lives to intercede" for believers, continually bringing their needs before the Father. As followers of Christ, believers are invited to participate in this ongoing work of intercession, praying for those who are in need, both spiritually and physically.

Intercession can take many forms:

1. Praying for the Lost: One of the most important aspects of intercession is praying for those who do not yet know Christ. As priests, believers are called to pray for the salvation of others, asking God to soften their hearts and open their eyes to the truth of the gospel. 2 Corinthians 4:4 reminds us that "the god of this age has blinded the minds of unbelievers," and it is through prayer that believers can ask God to break through that blindness and reveal His light to those in darkness.

2. Praying for Healing and Restoration: Just as Jesus healed the sick and restored the broken, believers are called to intercede for those who are suffering, whether physically, emotionally, or spiritually. James 5:16 encourages believers to "pray for each other so that you may be healed." Intercession involves asking God for His healing power to be released in the lives of those who are hurting, trusting that He is able to bring restoration and wholeness.

3. Praying for Leaders and Nations: 1 Timothy 2:2 specifically calls believers to intercede for "kings and all those in authority," so that "we may live peaceful and quiet lives in all godliness and holiness." As priests, believers have a responsibility to pray for their leaders, governments, and nations, asking God to grant wisdom, justice, and peace. Intercession for nations is a powerful way of partnering with God to bring about His kingdom on earth.

4. Praying for the Church: Interceding for fellow believers is another key part of the priestly ministry. Believers are called to pray for the growth, unity, and strength of the church, asking God to protect His people from spiritual attack and to equip them for the work of the ministry. Paul's prayers in his letters, such as in Ephesians 1:16-18, provide a model for interceding on behalf of the church, asking God to give

believers a deeper understanding of His love, wisdom, and power.

Intercession, then, is a powerful way in which believers exercise their priestly calling, standing in the gap for others and bringing their needs before the throne of grace. It is an act of love and service, reflecting the heart of God, who desires all people to be saved and come to the knowledge of the truth (1 Timothy 2:4).

Mediation and Reconciliation

In addition to interceding, believers are called to the ministry of mediation—helping to reconcile others to God. Just as Jesus is the ultimate mediator between God and humanity (1 Timothy 2:5), believers are invited to participate in this work of reconciliation by proclaiming the gospel and leading others to Christ.

The apostle Paul speaks of this priestly role of mediation in 2 Corinthians 5:18-20, where he writes:

> "All this is from God, who reconciled us to Himself through Christ and gave us the ministry of reconciliation: that God was reconciling the world to Himself in Christ, not counting people's sins against them. And He has committed to us the message of reconciliation. We are therefore Christ's ambassadors, as though God were making His appeal through us."

This passage reveals that God has entrusted believers with the "ministry of reconciliation," calling them to act as ambassadors for Christ. As priests, believers are tasked with sharing the message of reconciliation with the world, helping to bring others into right relationship with God through the gospel.

Mediation in this context involves:

1. Proclaiming the Gospel: The most important aspect of the ministry of reconciliation is sharing the good news of Jesus Christ. The gospel is the means by which people are reconciled to God, and as priests, believers are called to proclaim this message wherever they go. This may involve direct evangelism, teaching, or simply living out the gospel in a way that draws others to Christ. In Romans 10:14-15, Paul highlights the importance of this priestly role: "How, then, can they call on the one they have not believed in? And how can they believe in the one of whom they have not heard? And how can they hear without someone preaching to them?"

2. Guiding Others to Forgiveness: Mediation also involves helping others understand the forgiveness that is available through Christ. Many people live in guilt, shame, or condemnation, not realizing that Jesus has already made atonement for their sins. As priests, believers are called to lead others to the cross, where they can experience the full

forgiveness and grace of God. 1 John 1:9 assures us that "if we confess our sins, He is faithful and just and will forgive us our sins and purify us from all unrighteousness."

3. Helping Reconcile Relationships: In addition to reconciling people to God, believers are also called to help reconcile broken relationships between individuals. Jesus taught that peacemaking is a central part of the believer's life: "Blessed are the peacemakers, for they will be called children of God" (Matthew 5:9). As priests, believers can mediate in conflicts, offering wisdom, forgiveness, and grace to help restore broken relationships.

4. Representing Christ to the World: Mediation is not just about words; it is about living in a way that reflects Christ's love and grace to the world. Believers are called to be ambassadors of Christ, representing His kingdom values in their everyday lives. This means showing love, mercy, compassion, and forgiveness to those around them, just as Christ has shown these things to us. In Colossians 3:12-14, Paul writes, "Therefore, as God's chosen people, holy and dearly loved, clothe yourselves with compassion, kindness, humility, gentleness and patience. Bear with each other and forgive one another… And over all these virtues put on love, which binds them all together in perfect unity."

As priests, believers are called to embody the message of reconciliation in every aspect of their lives. By living out the gospel, they help mediate between God and a world that is in desperate need of His love and forgiveness.

The Power of Intercession and Mediation

Both intercession and mediation are powerful ways in which believers participate in God's redemptive work in the world. Intercession involves standing in the gap for others, praying for their needs and asking God to intervene in their lives. Mediation involves helping to reconcile others to God, whether through proclaiming the gospel, guiding others to forgiveness, or bringing healing to broken relationships.

The power of intercession and mediation is not in the individual believer's abilities but in the authority of Christ and the work of the Holy Spirit. As priests, believers are empowered by the Holy Spirit to pray effectively and to mediate reconciliation. Romans 8:26 assures us that the Holy Spirit helps us in our weakness, interceding for us with "groans that words cannot express." Similarly, the Spirit empowers believers to be ambassadors of Christ, giving them the boldness and wisdom they need to share the message of reconciliation.

The believer's role as a priest involves both intercession and mediation. Through intercession, believers stand in the gap for others, bringing their needs before God in prayer. Through mediation, believers help lead others to reconciliation with God, proclaiming the gospel and embodying the message of Christ in their daily lives. This priestly ministry is a powerful and essential part of the Christian life, reflecting the heart of God, who desires to bring healing, forgiveness, and restoration to the world.

As believers embrace their role as intercessors and mediators, they participate in God's ongoing work of redemption, advancing His kingdom and drawing others into His love and grace. In the next chapter, we will explore practical ways in which believers can live out their priestly calling, serving others, offering spiritual sacrifices, and making an impact for God's kingdom in their everyday lives.

Holiness and Service

Holiness is the hallmark of the priestly life and the foundation of a believer's calling as a royal priest. As priests in the New Covenant, believers are called to live lives that are set apart, reflecting God's character in their thoughts, words, and actions. This holiness is not a set of external religious rules but an internal transformation that results from a deep relationship with God. Flowing from this holiness is the believer's call to service, which is a practical expression of love for others and devotion to God. In this chapter, we explore how holiness and service define the believer's role as a priest and how these two elements are intertwined in living out the Christian life.

The Call to Holiness

Holiness is a defining characteristic of God and is one of the primary qualities that believers are called to embody in their priestly role. The call to holiness is both an invitation and a command. 1 Peter 1:15-16 states: "But just as He who called you is holy, so be holy in all you do; for it is written: 'Be holy, because I am holy.'" This call to holiness reflects the very nature of God, who is perfect, pure, and set apart from all sin and corruption. As believers, we are called to reflect this holiness in our own lives.

Holiness means being set apart for God's purposes. It involves living in a way that is distinct from the world, not conforming to its values or patterns but being transformed by the renewal of the mind (Romans 12:2). Holiness is not simply moral behavior; it is a way of life that is wholly dedicated to God, grounded in love for Him and a desire to walk in His ways. This inner transformation comes through the power of the Holy Spirit, who enables believers to live in holiness by changing their hearts and minds.

In the Old Testament, priests were set apart for service in the temple. They followed strict guidelines to remain ritually clean, reflecting the holiness required of them as mediators between God and the people. In the New Covenant, all believers are priests, and they are called to live in a similar state of holiness—not through external rituals but through a life marked by purity, integrity, and love for God.

Hebrews 12:14 reinforces this call: "Make every effort to live in peace with everyone and to be holy; without holiness no one will see the Lord." Holiness is not optional for the believer; it is a core aspect of the Christian life. However, it is important to recognize that holiness is not something believers can achieve on their own. It is the work of the Holy Spirit, who sanctifies believers and makes them more like Christ over time. 2 Corinthians 3:18 explains that "we are being transformed into His image with ever-increasing glory, which comes from the Lord, who is the Spirit."

Living a holy life involves:

1. Separation from Sin: As priests, believers are called to separate themselves from sin and live in righteousness. 1 John 3:9 declares, "No one who is born of God will continue to sin, because God's seed remains in them; they cannot go on sinning, because they have been born of God." While believers are not sinless, they are empowered by the Holy

Spirit to overcome sinful habits and to live in obedience to God's Word.

2. Pursuit of Righteousness: Holiness also involves an active pursuit of righteousness—living in a way that honors God and aligns with His will. Philippians 1:10-11 encourages believers to "be pure and blameless for the day of Christ, filled with the fruit of righteousness that comes through Jesus Christ." This means making choices that reflect God's character and seeking to grow in love, patience, kindness, and self-control.

3. Reflecting God's Character: As priests, believers are called to reflect God's holiness to the world. This means embodying the attributes of God in their daily lives—justice, mercy, truth, and love. Ephesians 4:24 instructs believers to "put on the new self, created to be like God in true righteousness and holiness." When believers live holy lives, they serve as a testimony to the world of God's transforming power and His desire for all people to be reconciled to Him.

Holiness Expressed Through Service

Holiness is not merely a personal, internal characteristic; it finds its practical expression in service to others. Just as Jesus, the ultimate High Priest, came "not to be served, but to serve" (Matthew 20:28), believers are called to follow His example by living lives of service, motivated by love. Service is one of the primary ways in which holiness is demonstrated in action. It reflects the selfless, sacrificial love of Christ and fulfills the greatest commandments to love God and love our neighbor (Matthew 22:37-39).

Service is an essential part of the priestly ministry. In the Old Testament, priests served the people by offering sacrifices, teaching the law, and caring for the temple. In the New Covenant, believers are called to serve others in a variety of ways, offering their time, talents, and resources to meet the needs of those around them and to advance God's kingdom.

Galatians 5:13 emphasizes this calling: "You, my brothers and sisters, were called to be free. But do not use your freedom to indulge the flesh; rather, serve one another humbly in love." Freedom in Christ is not a license for self-indulgence but an opportunity to serve others out of love. This service is a natural outflow of the holiness that believers are called to embody.

Service can take many forms, including:

1. Acts of Compassion: One of the most tangible ways to serve others is through acts of compassion and mercy. This can involve caring for the poor, feeding the hungry, visiting the sick, and comforting the brokenhearted. James 1:27 describes "pure and faultless" religion as "to look after orphans and widows in their distress." Service to the

marginalized and vulnerable is a direct reflection of God's heart for justice and mercy.

2. Using Spiritual Gifts: Every believer has been given spiritual gifts by the Holy Spirit for the purpose of serving the church and building up the body of Christ. 1 Peter 4:10 encourages believers to "use whatever gift you have received to serve others, as faithful stewards of God's grace in its various forms." Whether it's teaching, hospitality, leadership, or encouragement, believers are called to use their gifts in service to one another, helping the church grow and thrive.

3. Sharing the Gospel: One of the greatest acts of service a believer can offer is sharing the good news of Jesus Christ with others. As priests, believers are called to bring others into reconciliation with God, proclaiming the gospel and leading people to salvation. 2 Corinthians 5:20 describes believers as "ambassadors for Christ," carrying the message of reconciliation to a world in need. This act of service not only brings glory to God but also brings eternal life to those who hear and receive the gospel.

4. Serving in the Church and Community: Service is not limited to personal acts of kindness; it also involves participating in the life of the church and contributing to the well-being of the community. Believers are called to serve within the local church, supporting its ministries, encouraging

fellow believers, and helping to meet practical needs. At the same time, believers are called to engage with their broader community, serving as a light in the world and demonstrating the love of Christ in tangible ways.

Service as Worship

In the believer's priestly role, service is not just a duty but an act of worship. Just as Old Testament priests offered sacrifices in worship to God, New Testament believers are called to offer their lives as a "living sacrifice" (Romans 12:1), which includes acts of service. When believers serve others, they are ultimately serving God, reflecting His love and grace to those around them.

Hebrews 13:16 reminds believers, "Do not forget to do good and to share with others, for with such sacrifices God is pleased." Service, when motivated by love and humility, is pleasing to God and is a key part of the priestly calling. It is an expression of the believer's holiness, as they imitate Christ in His selfless love and care for others.

Service also has a transformative effect on the believer. As they give of themselves to others, they are drawn closer to God, experiencing the joy and fulfillment that comes from following Jesus' example. Mark 10:45 reminds us that "the Son of Man did not come to be served, but to serve," and as believers walk in this path of service, they grow in holiness and deepen their relationship with God.

Holiness and service are inseparable aspects of the believer's priestly life. Holiness reflects the internal transformation that takes place through the work of the Holy Spirit, setting believers apart for God's purposes and enabling them to live lives that reflect His character. Service is the practical expression of this holiness, as believers live out their calling to love and serve others in the name of Christ.

As priests in the New Covenant, believers are called to a life of holiness, marked by purity, integrity, and love for God. This holiness is lived out through acts of service, as believers use their gifts, resources, and time to care for others, advance God's kingdom, and proclaim the gospel. In doing so, they fulfill their priestly calling, offering their lives as living sacrifices, holy and pleasing to God.

In the next chapter, we will explore how believers can practically apply their roles as kings and priests in their daily lives, integrating holiness, service, spiritual authority, and intercession into the fabric of everyday living as they walk in their God-given calling.

CHAPTER 07

PRACTICAL APPLICATION IN DAILY LIFE

Leading with Integrity and Wisdom

As kings and priests in Christ, believers are not only given spiritual authority and the call to serve but are also entrusted with the responsibility to lead their lives and influence their surroundings with integrity and wisdom. In every sphere of life—whether in the home, workplace, church, or community—believers are called to embody the values of God's kingdom, making righteous decisions, serving as examples of godly character, and positively influencing others. This chapter explores how believers can practically apply their calling as leaders in their daily lives, leading with integrity and wisdom as they fulfill their role as kings under Christ.

Leading with Integrity

Integrity is at the heart of godly leadership. Integrity means living with consistency, honesty, and moral uprightness, aligning one's actions with God's truth and character. As kings, believers are called to lead their lives and their spheres of influence in a way that reflects the righteousness of God, walking in integrity in all they do.

Proverbs 10:9 states, "Whoever walks in integrity walks securely, but whoever takes crooked paths will be found out." This verse highlights the security and confidence that come from living a life of integrity. A leader who walks in integrity is trustworthy, dependable, and upright, building trust with others and serving as a reliable example of godly character.

Living with integrity means:

1. Being Honest and Transparent: A person of integrity is honest in their words and actions, even when it's difficult. They are transparent in their dealings with others and avoid deceit or manipulation. Proverbs 12:22 declares, "The Lord detests lying lips, but He delights in people who are trustworthy." In daily life, this means telling the truth, keeping commitments, and ensuring that one's words match their actions.

2. Making Ethical Decisions: Leading with integrity requires making decisions that align with God's moral

standards, even when those decisions come with personal cost. This may involve standing up for what is right, refusing to compromise on ethical issues, or choosing to do the right thing when others may not be watching. Proverbs 11:3 states, "The integrity of the upright guides them, but the unfaithful are destroyed by their duplicity." A leader of integrity follows the guidance of God's Word and resists the temptation to take shortcuts or engage in unethical behavior.

3. Being Faithful to Commitments: Integrity also involves faithfulness in fulfilling one's promises and responsibilities. Whether it's in a personal, professional, or spiritual context, a leader of integrity follows through on their commitments and takes responsibility for their actions. Psalm 15:4 describes the person who "keeps an oath even when it hurts," emphasizing the importance of faithfulness in every aspect of life.

4. Guarding Against Hypocrisy: Hypocrisy undermines integrity. A leader of integrity does not pretend to be something they are not or live a double life. Instead, they strive for authenticity, ensuring that their private life aligns with their public persona. James 1:22 warns against merely hearing the Word without acting on it, for this leads to self-deception. A leader with integrity practices what they preach, living out their faith consistently in all areas of life.

Integrity in leadership is vital because it fosters trust and respect from others. Whether in the workplace, church, family, or community, people are drawn to leaders who are trustworthy, authentic, and reliable. When believers lead with integrity, they not only build strong relationships but also serve as a reflection of Christ's character, pointing others to the source of their moral strength.

Leading with Wisdom

In addition to integrity, believers are called to lead with wisdom. Biblical wisdom goes beyond knowledge or intelligence; it is the ability to apply God's truth in practical ways, making decisions that reflect His will and bring about good outcomes. James 3:17 describes godly wisdom as "first of all pure; then peace-loving, considerate, submissive, full of mercy and good fruit, impartial and sincere." This wisdom is rooted in reverence for God and flows from a deep understanding of His Word.

Leading with wisdom involves:

1. Seeking God's Guidance: Wise leaders recognize their need for God's direction in every decision they make. Proverbs 3:5-6 instructs, "Trust in the Lord with all your heart and lean not on your own understanding; in all your ways submit to Him, and He will make your paths straight." This means prioritizing prayer and seeking God's will in decisions,

rather than relying solely on personal intuition or experience. In practical terms, this may involve asking God for wisdom in business decisions, relationships, or navigating difficult circumstances.

2. Using Discernment: Wisdom includes the ability to discern between right and wrong, good and evil, and the best course of action in a given situation. Philippians 1:9-10 encourages believers to "abound in knowledge and depth of insight," so that they may be able to "discern what is best." Discernment allows leaders to make decisions that are aligned with God's purposes and to avoid traps or compromises that would lead them astray. In daily life, discernment may involve assessing the motivations of others, evaluating the potential consequences of choices, or seeking wise counsel from trusted advisors.

3. Managing Resources Wisely: Leading with wisdom also involves being a good steward of the resources God has entrusted to believers—whether time, finances, or talents. Proverbs 21:5 teaches, "The plans of the diligent lead to profit as surely as haste leads to poverty." Wise leaders plan carefully, make prudent financial decisions, and invest their time and talents in ways that bring glory to God and benefit others. This stewardship applies to both personal life and

leadership responsibilities, ensuring that resources are used effectively for God's kingdom.

4. Promoting Peace and Unity: Wisdom is not only about making decisions but also about fostering peace and unity among those one leads. James 3:18 says, "Peacemakers who sow in peace reap a harvest of righteousness." A wise leader seeks to build harmony, resolve conflicts, and promote cooperation among individuals. In practical terms, this may involve mediating disputes, encouraging teamwork, or leading with a servant's heart that prioritizes the well-being of others.

5. Learning from Experience: Wisdom often comes through experience, both successes and failures. A wise leader is humble enough to learn from their mistakes and grow through difficult circumstances. Proverbs 9:9 says, "Instruct the wise and they will be wiser still; teach the righteous and they will add to their learning." This humility allows leaders to continually develop their skills and understanding, becoming more effective and compassionate in their leadership.

Influencing Others Positively

As kings in Christ's kingdom, believers are called to influence others in ways that reflect God's values and purposes. Leadership, at its core, is about influence—the ability to affect the behavior, attitudes, and actions of others. In their daily lives, believers have numerous opportunities to positively influence those around them, whether through their actions, words, or example.

1. Being a Godly Example: One of the most powerful ways believers can influence others is by being an example of godly character. 1 Timothy 4:12 encourages believers to "set an example for the believers in speech, in conduct, in love, in faith and in purity." When others see a believer living out their faith with integrity, love, and wisdom, it serves as a testimony to the power of God at work in their life. In practical terms, this may involve modeling patience in difficult situations, demonstrating kindness to those who are hurting, or showing generosity in times of need.

2. Encouraging and Building Others Up: Believers are called to encourage and build others up, helping them grow in their faith and fulfill their potential. 1 Thessalonians 5:11 instructs believers to "encourage one another and build each other up." This can be done through words of affirmation, acts of kindness, or providing guidance and mentorship. Positive influence means lifting others up, helping them see their worth in God's eyes, and encouraging them to pursue their God-given calling.

3. Sharing God's Wisdom: Leading with wisdom involves sharing that wisdom with others, offering insight and guidance when needed. Proverbs 27:9 says, "The heartfelt

counsel of a friend is as sweet as perfume and incense" (NLT). In daily life, this may mean offering advice to a friend, guiding a family member through a tough decision, or mentoring someone in the workplace. When believers lead with wisdom, they are able to influence others toward making righteous and godly decisions.

4. Standing for Justice and Truth: A kingly role involves standing for justice and truth, advocating for what is right in the face of injustice or dishonesty. Micah 6:8 reminds believers of their responsibility: "To act justly and to love mercy and to walk humbly with your God." In practical terms, this may involve speaking up against unfair treatment, supporting causes that align with God's heart for justice, or ensuring that one's own actions reflect fairness and integrity.

5. Creating a Positive Atmosphere: Believers can influence their environment by creating a positive, faith-filled atmosphere wherever they go. Proverbs 11:11 says, "Through the blessing of the upright a city is exalted." When believers speak words of life, bring joy to others, and demonstrate gratitude, they contribute to a culture that honors God. This could be as simple as offering a kind word, fostering a spirit of collaboration at work, or praying for those around them.

Leading with integrity and wisdom is central to the believer's role as a king under Christ. Integrity ensures that believers live in a way that reflects God's righteousness, building trust and demonstrating the power of a life rooted in truth. Wisdom enables believers to make decisions that honor God and lead to peace, unity, and growth. Together, these qualities allow believers to positively influence others, leading by example, encouraging those around them, and advancing God's kingdom in their daily lives.

In the next chapter, we will explore how believers can further integrate their roles as kings and priests by cultivating a lifestyle of spiritual authority, intercession, and service, fulfilling their God-given calling in every aspect of life.

Serving with Compassion and Humility

As priests in the New Covenant, believers are called to embody the heart of Christ by serving others with compassion and humility. This priestly service goes beyond religious duties; it encompasses meeting the practical needs of those around us, offering spiritual support, and demonstrating the love of Christ in tangible, everyday ways. Serving with compassion and humility is central to fulfilling the believer's priestly role, as it reflects Christ's own attitude of love and sacrificial service.

The Heart of Compassion

Compassion is a defining characteristic of Christ's ministry and should be reflected in the lives of His followers. Throughout the Gospels, Jesus is repeatedly described as being "moved with compassion" as He encounters the suffering, needs, and brokenness of people. Matthew 9:36 captures this heart of compassion: "When He saw the crowds, He had compassion on them, because they were harassed and helpless, like sheep without a shepherd." This same compassion is what drives believers to serve others in their time of need, recognizing the pain and struggles they face and responding with love.

Compassion involves entering into the suffering of others, feeling their pain, and being moved to action on their behalf. It is not merely an emotional response; it is love in action, meeting both the physical and spiritual needs of those around us.

Compassionate service includes:

1. Meeting Practical Needs: One of the most tangible ways believers can serve with compassion is by meeting the practical needs of others. This could involve providing food for the hungry, clothing for those in need, or shelter for the homeless. James 2:15-16 challenges believers to express their faith through practical action: "Suppose a brother or a sister is without clothes and daily food. If one of you says to them,

'Go in peace; keep warm and well fed,' but does nothing about their physical needs, what good is it?" Serving with compassion means not only recognizing the needs of others but taking steps to meet those needs in love.

2. Caring for the Vulnerable: Believers are called to show special care and attention to the vulnerable—those who are marginalized, oppressed, or in difficult situations. Isaiah 1:17 commands, "Learn to do good; seek justice, correct oppression; bring justice to the fatherless, plead the widow's cause." Whether it's advocating for justice, supporting those in crisis, or offering companionship to the lonely, serving with compassion involves lifting up the most vulnerable in society and standing with them in their struggles.

3. Offering Emotional and Spiritual Support: In addition to meeting physical needs, compassionate service includes offering emotional and spiritual support to those who are hurting. Galatians 6:2 encourages believers to "carry each other's burdens, and in this way you will fulfill the law of Christ." This might involve listening to someone's struggles, offering a word of encouragement, or praying with them during difficult times. Serving with compassion means being present with people in their pain and pointing them to the hope and comfort found in Christ.

4. Demonstrating Christ's Love in Action: Ultimately, compassionate service reflects the love of Christ. 1 John 3:18 urges believers to love "not with words or speech but with actions and in truth." As priests, believers are representatives of Christ's love to the world, and when they serve others with compassion, they reveal God's heart for the lost, the broken, and the suffering. This love in action is what distinguishes Christian service from mere humanitarian work—it flows from the love of God and seeks to glorify Him through acts of kindness and mercy.

The Attitude of Humility

While compassion drives believers to serve others, humility is the posture with which they are to serve. Humility is the quality of putting others' needs before one's own and serving without seeking recognition or reward. It is the mindset that Jesus Himself demonstrated throughout His ministry and most powerfully at the cross.

Philippians 2:5-7 provides a clear picture of Christ's humility: "In your relationships with one another, have the same mindset as Christ Jesus: who, being in very nature God, did not consider equality with God something to be used to His own advantage; rather, He made Himself nothing by taking the very nature of a servant." As priests, believers are called to adopt this same attitude, serving others selflessly and without seeking status or honor.

Humility in service includes:

1. Putting Others First: Serving with humility means prioritizing the needs of others above personal desires or convenience. Philippians 2:3-4 teaches, "Do nothing out of selfish ambition or vain conceit. Rather, in humility value others above yourselves, not looking to your own interests but each of you to the interests of the others." In daily life, this might involve sacrificing time, energy, or resources to help someone in need, even when it is inconvenient. It could also mean being willing to serve in unnoticed or unglamorous ways, knowing that God sees and values every act of service.

2. Serving Without Recognition: Humble service is not about receiving praise or recognition but about quietly fulfilling the work God has called believers to do. Matthew 6:1 warns, "Be careful not to practice your righteousness in front of others to be seen by them." Humility requires a willingness to serve in the background, without seeking the spotlight. It also involves being content with whatever role God assigns, whether it's leading or following, knowing that all service is valuable in His kingdom.

3. Serving as Jesus Served: Jesus provided the ultimate example of humble service when He washed His disciples'

feet, an act that was typically performed by the lowest of servants. John 13:14-15 recounts Jesus' words: "Now that I, your Lord and Teacher, have washed your feet, you also should wash one another's feet. I have set you an example that you should do as I have done for you." In following Christ's example, believers are called to serve one another in humility, even in tasks that might seem lowly or beneath them. This attitude of humility demonstrates the servant-heart of Jesus, who came to serve and not to be served (Mark 10:45).

4. Recognizing the Value of Every Person: Humility in service also involves recognizing the inherent value and dignity of every person, created in the image of God. This attitude drives believers to serve all people, regardless of their background, status, or circumstances. Romans 12:16 instructs believers to "live in harmony with one another" and "not be proud, but be willing to associate with people of low position." Serving with humility means treating every person with respect and love, seeing them as God sees them.

Demonstrating the Love of Christ

Serving with compassion and humility is a reflection of Christ's love, and it is through this kind of service that believers demonstrate the heart of God to the world. 1 Peter 4:10 reminds believers that each one "should use whatever gift you have received to serve others, as faithful stewards of

God's grace in its various forms." Service, when motivated by compassion and carried out with humility, becomes a powerful testimony of God's grace and love.

In practical terms, demonstrating the love of Christ through service means:

1. Serving Without Expectation: Christlike love is unconditional and self-giving. Believers are called to serve others without expecting anything in return—no recognition, reward, or reciprocation. Luke 6:35 encourages this kind of service: "Love your enemies, do good to them, and lend to them without expecting to get anything back." This selfless service reflects the love of Christ, who gave Himself for humanity without seeking personal gain.

2. Sharing in the Sufferings of Others: Compassionate and humble service involves walking alongside those who are suffering, sharing in their burdens and offering comfort. Romans 12:15 encourages believers to "rejoice with those who rejoice; mourn with those who mourn." This empathetic service demonstrates the love of Christ, who bore the burdens of others and calls His followers to do the same. It might mean sitting with someone in their grief, providing for their needs, or simply being a supportive presence.

3. Pointing Others to Christ: Ultimately, the goal of serving with compassion and humility is to point others to

Jesus. Whether through meeting practical needs, offering spiritual support, or demonstrating kindness, believers have the opportunity to direct others toward the source of their love and service—Jesus Christ. Matthew 5:16 reminds believers to "let your light shine before others, that they may see your good deeds and glorify your Father in heaven." Service is a form of evangelism, revealing the heart of God to a world in need of His grace.

Serving with compassion and humility is an essential part of the believer's priestly role in the New Covenant. Compassion drives believers to meet the practical and spiritual needs of those around them, reflecting the heart of Christ. Humility ensures that this service is selfless, putting others first and seeking to glorify God rather than self. Together, compassion and humility form the foundation of Christlike service, allowing believers to demonstrate the love of God in tangible ways.

As priests, believers are called to serve those in need, lift up the vulnerable, offer spiritual and emotional support, and point others to Christ through their actions. By following the example of Jesus, who served with compassion and humility, believers fulfill their calling to be representatives of God's grace and love in the world.

Declaring God's Praises

One of the most profound responsibilities of the royal priesthood is to declare the praises of God. This is an essential aspect of a believer's identity as both king and priest in the kingdom of God. As priests, believers are called to testify of God's goodness, share their faith, and worship Him both privately and publicly. Declaring God's praises is not only about worship in the traditional sense but also about living a life that continually reflects and proclaims the greatness of God to the world. In this chapter, we will explore the biblical foundation for this calling and how believers can practically live it out in their daily lives.

The Biblical Call to Declare God's Praises

The call to declare the praises of God is deeply rooted in Scripture. 1 Peter 2:9 encapsulates this calling: "But you are a chosen people, a royal priesthood, a holy nation, God's special possession, that you may declare the praises of Him who called you out of darkness into His wonderful light." This verse highlights the believer's identity and purpose. God has set His people apart to proclaim His greatness, to tell the world about the life-transforming power of His grace, and to worship Him in all circumstances.

This declaration is not limited to singing songs or speaking praises in a formal setting. It is a lifestyle of continually pointing to God's goodness in every situation. Believers are to be living testimonies of God's faithfulness, mercy, and power. Through their words, actions, and attitudes, they are called to make God known, bringing glory to His name in all they do.

Psalm 145:4-7 reflects the heart of this calling: "One generation commends Your works to another; they tell of Your mighty acts. They speak of the glorious splendor of Your majesty—and I will meditate on Your wonderful works. They tell of the power of Your awesome works—and I will proclaim Your great deeds. They celebrate Your abundant goodness and joyfully sing of Your righteousness." As believers declare the praises of God, they contribute to the ongoing testimony of His work across generations, keeping the story of God's salvation alive.

Testifying of God's Goodness

One of the primary ways believers declare God's praises is through testifying of His goodness. Testimonies are powerful because they are personal accounts of how God has worked in someone's life, and they offer undeniable evidence of His love, grace, and power. Revelation 12:11 says, "They triumphed over [the enemy] by the blood of the Lamb and by the word of their testimony." This highlights the importance of sharing our faith experiences with others—it strengthens faith, encourages fellow believers, and bears witness to the world of God's reality.

Testifying of God's goodness can take many forms:

1. Sharing Personal Testimonies: Every believer has a unique story of how God has worked in their life. Whether it's a testimony of salvation, healing, provision, or transformation, these stories are powerful tools for declaring God's praises. When believers share their personal testimonies, they give glory to God and show others what He is capable of doing. Psalm 107:2 says, "Let the redeemed of the Lord tell their story." In daily life, this may involve sharing one's testimony with a friend, family member, or coworker who is struggling, or giving thanks to God in a public setting for a blessing or answered prayer.

2. Celebrating God's Faithfulness: Declaring God's praises also involves celebrating His faithfulness in everyday life. When believers recognize and acknowledge the ways God has provided, protected, and guided them, they are testifying of His ongoing involvement in their lives. This could be as simple as thanking God for answered prayers, sharing a blessing with others, or publicly acknowledging His hand in both big and small moments. Psalm 66:16 invites us to "Come and hear, all you who fear God; let me tell you what He has done for me."

3. Sharing the Gospel: The ultimate testimony of God's goodness is the gospel of Jesus Christ. As priests, believers are called to proclaim the good news of salvation to those who have not yet heard. Romans 10:14 reminds us of the importance of this task: "How, then, can they call on the one they have not believed in? And how can they believe in the one of whom they have not heard? And how can they hear without someone preaching to them?" Sharing the gospel is an act of declaring God's praises, telling the world of the greatest act of love and mercy—the life, death, and resurrection of Jesus Christ.

Public and Private Worship

Worship is at the heart of declaring God's praises. While worship can take many forms, it is ultimately an expression of reverence, love, and adoration for God. Believers are called to worship God both privately in their personal devotion and publicly as part of the body of Christ. Worship is more than just singing songs; it is a lifestyle of giving glory to God in all things.

1. Private Worship: Private worship is an essential part of a believer's life, as it fosters intimacy with God and keeps one's heart aligned with Him. Matthew 6:6 encourages believers to pray and seek God in the "secret place," where they can have personal communion with Him. Private

worship may include personal prayer, meditation on Scripture, singing praises, or simply spending quiet time in God's presence. This daily discipline helps believers grow in their relationship with God and equips them to declare His praises publicly.

Psalm 63:1 reflects the heart of private worship: "You, God, are my God, earnestly I seek you; I thirst for you, my whole being longs for you, in a dry and parched land where there is no water." In private worship, believers draw near to God, expressing their love for Him and acknowledging His greatness.

2. Public Worship: While private worship is crucial, believers are also called to join together in public worship, where they corporately declare the praises of God. Hebrews 10:25 reminds believers "not to give up meeting together," for there is power in collective worship. When the body of Christ comes together to lift up the name of God, they create a powerful atmosphere of praise that glorifies God and encourages one another.

Psalm 100:4 calls believers to "enter His gates with thanksgiving and His courts with praise." Public worship includes participating in church services, corporate prayer meetings, and other gatherings where believers collectively worship God. This public expression of worship not only strengthens the faith community but also serves as a witness to the world of God's glory.

Living a Life of Worship

Declaring God's praises is not limited to moments of worship or testimony; it is about living a life that consistently reflects His greatness. Colossians 3:17 urges believers, "And whatever you do, whether in word or deed, do it all in the name of the Lord Jesus, giving thanks to God the Father through Him." This means that everything believers do—whether at work, home, or church—should be done with an attitude of worship, gratitude, and praise.

Living a life of worship involves:

1. Honoring God in Everyday Life: Worship is not just something that happens on Sunday mornings; it is an everyday reality. Believers declare God's praises by living in a way that honors Him in their relationships, work, and interactions with others. Romans 12:1 calls believers to "offer your bodies as a living sacrifice, holy and pleasing to God—this is your true and proper worship." This means that everything believers do should be done with the intention of glorifying God, whether it's how they treat their family, how they work, or how they speak to others.

2. Practicing Gratitude: A lifestyle of worship includes practicing gratitude in all circumstances. 1 Thessalonians 5:18

commands, "Give thanks in all circumstances; for this is God's will for you in Christ Jesus." When believers cultivate an attitude of thankfulness, they are continually declaring God's praises, recognizing His goodness in every situation. Gratitude shifts the focus from one's own struggles to God's faithfulness and provision.

3. Living Out the Fruit of the Spirit: Another way to declare God's praises is by living in such a way that reflects the fruit of the Spirit—love, joy, peace, patience, kindness, goodness, faithfulness, gentleness, and self-control (Galatians 5:22-23). When believers exhibit these qualities in their daily lives, they are living testimonies of God's transforming power. The way believers interact with others, handle difficult situations, and respond to adversity can all serve as declarations of God's grace and goodness.

4. Serving Others: Finally, serving others is a form of worship that declares God's praises. When believers serve those in need, they are reflecting the heart of Christ and showing the world what God's love looks like in action. Matthew 5:16 encourages believers to "let your light shine before others, that they may see your good deeds and glorify your Father in heaven." Acts of service—whether helping a neighbor, volunteering at church, or supporting a friend in need—are all ways to declare the greatness of God.

Declaring the praises of God is a key aspect of the believer's identity as part of the royal priesthood. Whether through sharing testimonies, engaging in private and public worship, or living a life that reflects God's character,

believers are called to make God known in every aspect of their lives. Testifying of God's goodness, sharing the gospel, and living with an attitude of worship are all ways that believers fulfill their priestly role, bringing glory to God and shining His light in the world.

CHAPTER 08

THE CHURCH AS A ROYAL PRIESTHOOD

Corporate Identity and Unity

The concept of the royal priesthood is not only an individual calling for believers but also a corporate identity for the church as a collective body of Christ. As a royal priesthood, the church is set apart by God to serve Him and represent His kingdom on earth. This corporate identity emphasizes that believers are not meant to function in isolation but in unity with one another, working together to fulfill their priestly roles. Unity among believers is essential for effective ministry and witness, and this unity is built on shared faith, love, and purpose. In this chapter, we explore the biblical foundation of the church as a royal priesthood, the importance of unity, and how the church can live out its collective calling in the world.

The Biblical Foundation of the Royal Priesthood

The idea of the church as a royal priesthood is rooted in Scripture, where the people of God are described not only as individuals who serve Him but as a unified, holy nation. 1 Peter 2:9 lays the foundation for this identity: "But you are a chosen people, a royal priesthood, a holy nation, God's special possession, that you may declare the praises of Him who called you out of darkness into His wonderful light." This passage highlights that the royal priesthood is not just a personal role but a collective calling for the church to embody God's purposes on earth.

The language of priesthood in Exodus 19:6 further supports this corporate identity: "You will be for me a kingdom of priests and a holy nation." God's intention for Israel was that the entire nation would serve as priests, representing His presence to the nations. Similarly, in the New Covenant, the church fulfills this priestly role by being a light to the world, offering spiritual sacrifices, and advancing God's kingdom.

This corporate priesthood means that the church is tasked with interceding for the world, proclaiming the gospel, worshiping God together, and serving in ways that reflect Christ's love and grace. Every believer plays a role in this, but it is the collective unity of the church that makes this mission powerful and effective.

The Importance of Unity in the Church

Unity among believers is critical for the church to fulfill its calling as a royal priesthood. Without unity, the church becomes divided, distracted, and ineffective in its ministry and witness. Jesus Himself emphasized the importance of unity in His prayer for His disciples in John 17:20-23: "I pray also for those who will believe in Me through their message, that all of them may be one, Father, just as You are in Me and I am in You... Then the world will know that You sent Me and have loved them even as You have loved Me."

This prayer highlights that unity within the church is not just for the sake of harmony but serves as a witness to the world of God's love and the truth of the gospel. When the church is united, it reflects the unity within the Godhead— the relationship between the Father, Son, and Holy Spirit— and becomes a living testimony to God's power and purpose.

Unity in the church is built on several key foundations:

1. Shared Faith in Christ: The cornerstone of unity is a shared faith in Jesus Christ. Ephesians 4:4-6 declares, "There is one body and one Spirit, just as you were called to one hope when you were called; one Lord, one faith, one baptism; one

God and Father of all, who is over all and through all and in all." Regardless of differences in background, culture, or denomination, all believers are united by their faith in Christ as Lord and Savior. This shared faith is the foundation of the church's unity and the basis for working together in ministry.

2. Love for One Another: Unity in the church is sustained by love. Colossians 3:14 teaches, "And over all these virtues put on love, which binds them all together in perfect unity." Love is the glue that holds the body of Christ together, enabling believers to serve one another, forgive offenses, and work through differences. Jesus commanded His followers to "love one another" as a demonstration of their discipleship (John 13:34-35). When the church operates in love, it creates an environment where unity can thrive, and the collective priesthood can function effectively.

3. A Common Purpose: The church's unity is also built on a shared purpose—to glorify God, spread the gospel, and make disciples. Philippians 2:2 encourages believers to be "like-minded, having the same love, being one in spirit and of one mind." This common mission gives the church a sense of direction and focus, ensuring that all efforts and ministries are working toward the same goal. When believers are united around this purpose, they can collaborate more effectively,

combining their gifts and resources to advance God's kingdom.

4. Mutual Submission and Humility: For unity to flourish in the church, there must be an attitude of mutual submission and humility. Ephesians 5:21 instructs believers to "submit to one another out of reverence for Christ." This means putting the needs of others before personal preferences, being willing to listen, and valuing the perspectives and contributions of fellow believers. Philippians 2:3 calls believers to "do nothing out of selfish ambition or vain conceit. Rather, in humility value others above yourselves." Humility is essential for maintaining unity, as it enables believers to serve together without competition or division.

Living Out the Royal Priesthood in Unity

To live out the collective calling of the royal priesthood, the church must actively pursue unity and seek ways to work together in ministry and witness. This involves both corporate worship and practical acts of service that reflect the love and grace of God to the world.

1. Corporate Worship: Worship is one of the most powerful ways the church can express its unity as a royal priesthood. When believers gather together to worship God, they are fulfilling their priestly role by offering spiritual

sacrifices of praise and thanksgiving. Hebrews 10:24-25 emphasizes the importance of gathering together: "And let us consider how we may spur one another on toward love and good deeds, not giving up meeting together, as some are in the habit of doing, but encouraging one another."

Corporate worship allows believers to unite their voices and hearts in adoration of God, creating an atmosphere of unity and strengthening the bond between members of the body. It is a visible demonstration of the church's unity and a foretaste of the eternal worship that will take place in heaven.

2. Collaborative Ministry: The church as a royal priesthood is also called to work together in ministry, using the diverse gifts and talents of its members to serve others and advance God's kingdom. 1 Corinthians 12:12 describes the church as a body made up of many parts, each with a unique function but all working together for the common good. When the church operates in unity, each member contributes to the whole, and the collective ministry is more effective.

This collaborative ministry may include evangelism, community outreach, discipleship, and acts of mercy. Whether it's caring for the poor, supporting missionaries, or teaching the next generation, the church's unity enables it to accomplish far more together than any individual could achieve alone.

3. Intercession and Prayer: As part of the royal priesthood, the church is called to intercede on behalf of the world, praying for God's will to be done on earth as it is in heaven. 1 Timothy 2:1 encourages believers to "make petitions, prayers, intercession and thanksgiving for all people." Corporate prayer is a powerful expression of the church's unity, as believers come together to seek God's guidance, pray for one another, and intercede for the needs of the world.

Through prayer, the church exercises its priestly authority, standing in the gap for those who do not yet know Christ and asking God to bring healing, justice, and salvation to the world.

4. Serving the Community: Unity in the church is also expressed through serving the community. The church is called to be a light in the world, reflecting the love of Christ through acts of service and compassion. Matthew 5:14-16 reminds believers that they are the "light of the world" and encourages them to "let your light shine before others, that they may see your good deeds and glorify your Father in heaven."

Whether it's feeding the hungry, caring for the sick, or advocating for justice, the church's unity in service makes a tangible impact on the world and bears witness to the transformative power of the gospel. By working together to meet the needs of the community, the church demonstrates the love of Christ and fulfills its priestly role.

Overcoming Obstacles to Unity

While unity is essential for the church's effectiveness, it is not always easy to achieve. Differences in opinion, personality, culture, and background can create barriers to unity. However, the church is called to actively pursue unity and overcome these obstacles through grace, forgiveness, and love.

1. Dealing with Conflict: Conflict is inevitable in any community, but how the church handles conflict can either strengthen or weaken its unity. Matthew 18:15-17 provides a biblical framework for resolving conflict, encouraging believers to address issues directly and seek reconciliation. Forgiveness is also a key component of maintaining unity. Colossians 3:13 urges believers to "bear with each other and forgive one another if any of you has a grievance against someone."

2. Promoting Inclusivity: The church is called to be inclusive, welcoming people from all backgrounds, cultures,

and walks of life. Galatians 3:28 reminds us, "There is neither Jew nor Gentile, neither slave nor free, nor is there male and female, for you are all one in Christ Jesus." This means embracing diversity within the body of Christ and celebrating the different gifts and perspectives each member brings.

3. Cultivating a Spirit of Humility: Finally, unity requires humility. Ephesians 4:2-3 encourages believers to "be completely humble and gentle; be patient, bearing with one another in love. Make every effort to keep the unity of the Spirit through the bond of peace." By cultivating a spirit of humility, believers can serve one another in love and prioritize the well-being of the community over individual preferences.

The church, as a royal priesthood, is called to embody unity, working together to fulfill God's mission on earth. This unity is built on shared faith, love for one another, and a common purpose to glorify God and make His kingdom known. When the church operates in unity, it becomes a powerful witness to the world, demonstrating the love, grace, and truth of Christ.

Through corporate worship, collaborative ministry, intercession, and acts of service, the church lives out its collective identity as a royal priesthood. By overcoming obstacles to unity and cultivating a spirit of humility, the church can continue to grow in its effectiveness and impact, advancing God's kingdom and bringing glory to His name.

In the next chapter, we will explore how believers can further cultivate their roles as kings and priests by growing in spiritual authority, deepening their prayer lives, and engaging in the ministry of reconciliation, continuing to fulfill the high calling of representing Christ to the world.

Ministry and Mission of the Church

The church is not just a gathering of believers but a body called to mission—proclaiming the gospel, making disciples, and serving the community. Every believer, as part of the royal priesthood, has a significant role in fulfilling this mission. The ministry and mission of the church are rooted in Christ's Great Commission and the call to be His representatives in the world. In this chapter, we will explore how the church collectively fulfills its mission and how each believer contributes to this purpose.

The Great Commission: Proclaiming the Gospel

The church's mission is founded on the command of Jesus in the Great Commission. Matthew 28:19-20 outlines this central purpose: "Therefore go and make disciples of all nations, baptizing them in the name of the Father and of the Son and of the Holy Spirit, and teaching them to obey everything I have commanded you." This commission to proclaim the gospel and make disciples is the heartbeat of the church's mission.

The church is called to bring the good news of Jesus Christ to the world, sharing the message of salvation, forgiveness, and reconciliation with God. This involves both evangelism—sharing the gospel with those who have not yet heard or believed—and discipleship—teaching and equipping believers to grow in their faith and follow Christ more closely.

1. Evangelism: Proclaiming the gospel is at the core of the church's mission. Romans 10:14-15 asks, "How, then, can they call on the one they have not believed in? And how can they believe in the one of whom they have not heard? And how can they hear without someone preaching to them?" The church is called to be the voice of God's truth in the world, spreading the message of Christ through words and actions. Evangelism can take many forms, from personal conversations and testimonies to organized outreach efforts, media, and missions work. Every believer is called to be a witness to the power of the gospel, sharing their faith with others and inviting them to know Christ.

2. Discipleship: Once individuals come to faith in Christ, the church's role extends to discipling them—helping them grow in their understanding of the Bible, develop a

deeper relationship with God, and live out their faith. Matthew 28:20 calls the church to "teach them to obey everything I have commanded you." This discipleship process involves teaching, mentoring, and walking alongside new believers as they mature in their faith. Discipleship is not just about knowledge but about transformation—helping believers become more like Christ in their character, actions, and relationships.

In fulfilling the Great Commission, the church takes part in God's redemptive plan for humanity, bringing the light of Christ into a dark world. This mission is not confined to the church building; it is a global mandate to reach people of every nation, tribe, and tongue with the life-saving message of the gospel.

The Ministry of Making Disciples

Making disciples is not just about bringing people to faith but about equipping them to live out their calling as followers of Christ. This process of discipleship is a lifelong journey that involves growth, accountability, and transformation. The ministry of the church is to nurture and develop believers into mature, equipped disciples who can, in turn, disciple others.

1. Teaching and Preaching: One of the primary ways the church fulfills its discipleship mandate is through teaching

and preaching the Word of God. 2 Timothy 3:16-17 emphasizes the importance of Scripture in the process of discipleship: "All Scripture is God-breathed and is useful for teaching, rebuking, correcting, and training in righteousness, so that the servant of God may be thoroughly equipped for every good work." Through sermons, Bible studies, and small groups, the church provides believers with the knowledge and tools they need to grow in their faith.

2. Mentoring and Accountability: Discipleship is not just about imparting knowledge; it is also about walking alongside others in their spiritual journey. Proverbs 27:17 states, "As iron sharpens iron, so one person sharpens another." The church encourages believers to mentor one another, offering guidance, support, and accountability in their spiritual growth. This mentoring can take place in formal discipleship programs or through informal relationships where believers encourage one another to live according to God's Word.

3. Spiritual Growth and Maturity: The goal of discipleship is spiritual maturity—developing believers who are grounded in their faith and able to live as faithful followers of Christ. Ephesians 4:13 calls believers to "reach unity in the faith and in the knowledge of the Son of God and become mature, attaining to the whole measure of the fullness of

Christ." This maturity is evidenced by a deepening relationship with God, a growing understanding of Scripture, and the development of Christlike character. The church's ministry is to create an environment where believers can grow in their faith, develop their spiritual gifts, and be equipped to serve others.

4. Multiplication: A key aspect of discipleship is multiplication—disciples making disciples. 2 Timothy 2:2 emphasizes the importance of passing on what has been learned: "And the things you have heard me say in the presence of many witnesses entrust to reliable people who will also be qualified to teach others." The church's mission is not complete until disciples are equipped to disciple others, creating a cycle of growth and multiplication that extends the reach of the gospel.

Serving the Community

The church's mission goes beyond evangelism and discipleship; it also includes serving the community and meeting the practical needs of those around them. Jesus modeled this aspect of ministry throughout His life, caring for the poor, healing the sick, and demonstrating compassion to those in need. The church, as the body of Christ, is called to continue this ministry of service, reflecting God's love through acts of compassion and justice.

1. Caring for the Needy: James 1:27 defines "pure and faultless" religion as caring "for orphans and widows in their distress." The church is called to care for the most vulnerable members of society, providing for their needs and offering hope and support in times of distress. This includes feeding the hungry, clothing the poor, visiting the sick, and supporting those who are marginalized or oppressed. By serving the community in these tangible ways, the church demonstrates the love of Christ in action.

2. Advocating for Justice: The church's mission also involves advocating for justice and working to bring about systemic change in the world. Micah 6:8 calls believers to "act justly and to love mercy and to walk humbly with your God." This means standing up for the oppressed, fighting against injustice, and seeking to bring about peace and reconciliation in a broken world. Whether through community outreach, social justice initiatives, or partnerships with local organizations, the church has a role in advocating for the well-being of all people.

3. Building Strong Communities: The church is also called to contribute to the overall health and well-being of the community. This may involve providing educational programs, offering counseling services, supporting families, or engaging in efforts to promote social and economic

development. Jeremiah 29:7 encourages believers to "seek the peace and prosperity of the city" in which they live. By investing in the community, the church helps create environments where people can thrive and experience the love and grace of God.

4. Demonstrating the Kingdom of God: Ultimately, the church's mission of service is about demonstrating the kingdom of God. Matthew 5:16 encourages believers to "let your light shine before others, that they may see your good deeds and glorify your Father in heaven." When the church serves the community, it reflects the values of God's kingdom—love, justice, mercy, and compassion—and points people to the hope and salvation found in Jesus Christ.

Every Believer's Role in the Mission

As part of the royal priesthood, every believer has a role in fulfilling the mission of the church. The mission is not just for pastors or church leaders; it is the calling of all believers to participate in proclaiming the gospel, making disciples, and serving the community. Ephesians 4:11-12 explains that church leaders are to "equip His people for works of service, so that the body of Christ may be built up." This means that each believer is to be equipped and empowered to live out their priestly calling in their everyday life.

1. Using Spiritual Gifts: Every believer has been given spiritual gifts by the Holy Spirit to contribute to the mission of the church. 1 Peter 4:10 reminds believers to "use whatever gift you have received to serve others, as faithful stewards of God's grace." These gifts may include teaching, evangelism, administration, hospitality, mercy, or leadership. By using their gifts, believers play an active role in advancing the church's mission and building up the body of Christ.

2. Living as a Witness: Every believer is called to be a witness to the world, sharing their faith and living in a way that reflects the character of Christ. Acts 1:8 promises, "But you will receive power when the Holy Spirit comes on you; and you will be My witnesses in Jerusalem, and in all Judea and Samaria, and to the ends of the earth." Witnessing is not limited to words; it involves living a life that testifies to God's goodness and grace in both big and small ways.

3. Serving in the Church and Beyond: Every believer has the opportunity to serve within the local church and beyond. This may involve volunteering in a ministry, mentoring new believers, participating in outreach efforts, or supporting missions work. 1 Corinthians 12:27 reminds us that "you are the body of Christ, and each one of you is a part of it." The church thrives when every member contributes their time, talent, and resources to the mission.

The ministry and mission of the church are rooted in the Great Commission and the call to be a royal priesthood. Proclaiming the gospel, making disciples, and serving the community are central to this mission, and every believer has a role to play in fulfilling it. Whether through evangelism, discipleship, acts of service, or community engagement, the church is called to be the hands and feet of Christ in the world.

As believers embrace their role in the royal priesthood, they contribute to the advancement of God's kingdom and help others experience the transforming power of the gospel. In the next chapter, we will explore how believers can grow in spiritual authority and deepen their relationship with God, empowering them to live out their priestly and kingly roles with greater impact and effectiveness.

Impact on Society

The Royal Priesthood: A Transformative Presence in Society

As members of the royal priesthood, believers are called not only to serve within the church but to be a transformative presence in society. By living out their God-given identity, believers can influence culture, advocate for justice, and contribute to the common good. The impact of the church extends beyond the walls of the sanctuary and into every corner of society, as believers bring the values of the kingdom of God to bear on the world around them. In this chapter, we will explore how the royal priesthood is called to shape culture, pursue justice, and work for the flourishing of all people.

Influencing Culture as a Royal Priesthood

As followers of Christ, believers are called to be salt and light in the world, influencing the culture around them by reflecting the values of God's kingdom. Matthew 5:13-16 outlines this calling: "You are the salt of the earth… You are the light of the world. A town built on a hill cannot be hidden." Salt preserves and flavors, while light illuminates and guides. In the same way, believers are called to preserve what is good in society, offer a countercultural witness, and shine the light of Christ in every area of life.

1. Living Out Kingdom Values: One of the primary ways believers can influence culture is by living out the values of the kingdom of God in their everyday lives. This includes practicing love, humility, forgiveness, generosity, and compassion. As believers embody these virtues, they serve as a living testimony to the transformative power of the gospel. In a world that often promotes self-interest, competition, and division, the royal priesthood is called to model a different

way of living—one that reflects the character of Christ and points others to Him.

2. Engaging in the Arts, Media, and Education: Another way the royal priesthood can influence culture is by engaging in fields such as the arts, media, and education. These sectors have a profound impact on shaping public opinion, values, and beliefs. By participating in these areas, believers have the opportunity to create content, shape narratives, and influence thought in ways that reflect biblical truth. Whether it's producing films, writing books, or teaching in schools, Christians can use their platforms to present a worldview that honors God and uplifts humanity.

3. Contributing to Public Discourse: Believers are also called to contribute to public discourse on important issues affecting society. Colossians 4:6 encourages believers to "let your conversation be always full of grace, seasoned with salt, so that you may know how to answer everyone." By engaging thoughtfully and respectfully in discussions on social, political, and ethical matters, believers can offer wisdom and insight rooted in biblical principles. This may involve participating in community forums, writing opinion pieces, or simply having conversations with friends and colleagues. The goal is not to dominate but to contribute meaningfully,

helping shape a culture that aligns with the values of God's kingdom.

4. Being a Witness in the Workplace: The workplace is another important arena where believers can influence culture. By demonstrating integrity, fairness, diligence, and kindness, Christians can make a positive impact on their work environments. Colossians 3:23 reminds believers, "Whatever you do, work at it with all your heart, as working for the Lord, not for human masters." This approach to work sets believers apart and reflects the high standards of God's kingdom. Whether in leadership positions or entry-level roles, believers can model Christlike character and inspire others to pursue excellence and compassion in their professional lives.

Advocating for Justice

As members of the royal priesthood, believers are also called to advocate for justice and work toward a society that reflects God's heart for righteousness and fairness. Micah 6:8 expresses this calling clearly: "He has shown you, O mortal, what is good. And what does the Lord require of you? To act justly and to love mercy and to walk humbly with your God." Justice, mercy, and humility are key elements of the believer's role in society.

1. Pursuing Social Justice: Advocating for justice involves addressing the root causes of injustice in society and

working to correct systemic issues that lead to inequality, oppression, and exploitation. Proverbs 31:8-9 instructs believers to "speak up for those who cannot speak for themselves, for the rights of all who are destitute. Speak up and judge fairly; defend the rights of the poor and needy." This may involve supporting policies that promote justice, working with organizations that fight poverty or human trafficking, or volunteering in initiatives that seek to address homelessness or provide legal aid to marginalized communities.

2. Defending the Vulnerable: Throughout Scripture, God shows a particular concern for the vulnerable—the poor, the widow, the orphan, and the foreigner. As a royal priesthood, the church is called to reflect God's compassion by defending and supporting those who are most at risk in society. Isaiah 1:17 calls believers to "learn to do right; seek justice. Defend the oppressed. Take up the cause of the fatherless; plead the case of the widow." This advocacy can take many forms, from supporting local food banks and shelters to standing up for the rights of refugees and immigrants. It may also involve working to eliminate exploitation and discrimination in areas such as employment, education, and housing.

3. Promoting Peace and Reconciliation: The church is also called to be a peacemaker in society, promoting peace and reconciliation in a world often torn by conflict and division. Matthew 5:9 says, "Blessed are the peacemakers, for they will be called children of God." Whether in personal relationships, community disputes, or broader social tensions, believers are called to be agents of peace, seeking reconciliation and unity where there is discord. This can involve mediating conflicts, participating in peace-building efforts, or advocating for nonviolent solutions to societal problems.

4. Standing for Truth and Righteousness: Advocating for justice also means standing for truth and righteousness, even when it is unpopular. Ephesians 5:11 instructs believers to "have nothing to do with the fruitless deeds of darkness, but rather expose them." This may involve speaking out against corruption, injustice, or unethical practices in business, government, or other institutions. Believers are called to be voices for truth, challenging systems and behaviors that undermine justice and righteousness in society.

Contributing to the Common Good

In addition to influencing culture and advocating for justice, the royal priesthood is called to contribute to the common good, working for the flourishing of all people and promoting the well-being of society as a whole. This calling is grounded in the biblical principle of loving one's neighbor and seeking the welfare of the community.

1. Serving the Community: One of the most practical ways believers can contribute to the common good is by serving their communities. Jeremiah 29:7 encourages believers to "seek the peace and prosperity of the city to which I have carried you into exile. Pray to the Lord for it, because if it prospers, you too will prosper." By investing in the well-being of their cities and neighborhoods, Christians can create spaces where people can thrive physically, emotionally, and spiritually. This may involve volunteering at local schools, supporting community health initiatives, or participating in environmental sustainability efforts.

2. Promoting Human Dignity: The royal priesthood is also called to promote the inherent dignity of every human being, recognizing that all people are created in the image of God (Genesis 1:27). This means working to ensure that all people have access to basic needs such as food, water, shelter, healthcare, and education. It also means standing against dehumanizing practices such as racism, sexism, and other forms of discrimination. By affirming the worth of every individual, the church can contribute to a society where all people are treated with respect and love.

3. Encouraging Civic Responsibility: Believers can contribute to the common good by participating in civic life and encouraging others to do the same. Romans 13:1 calls believers to submit to governing authorities and participate in the structures that promote order and justice. This may involve voting in elections, advocating for policies that promote the welfare of society, or serving in public office. By engaging in civic responsibilities, believers can help shape a society that reflects the values of God's kingdom.

4. Creating Opportunities for Flourishing: Finally, the royal priesthood is called to create opportunities for human flourishing by promoting education, economic empowerment, and innovation. Proverbs 11:10 says, "When the righteous prosper, the city rejoices." By using their talents, resources, and influence to create jobs, support local businesses, or mentor young people, believers can help others reach their full potential and contribute to the well-being of society. Whether in business, education, healthcare, or the arts, Christians can use their skills to build up their communities and create environments where all people can flourish.

As a royal priesthood, the church is called to be a transformative presence in society, influencing culture, advocating for justice, and contributing to the common good.

By living out their identity in Christ, believers can make a profound impact on the world around them, bringing the values of God's kingdom into every sphere of life. Through acts of service, advocacy for justice, and participation in community life, the church can reflect the love, truth, and righteousness of God, shaping a society that honors Him and promotes human flourishing

CHAPTER 09

CHALLENGES AND RESPONSIBILITIES

Overcoming Spiritual Battles

Living out the identity of kings and priests in Christ brings both tremendous privileges and significant responsibilities. One of the most critical aspects of this calling involves engaging in spiritual battles. As believers seek to live in accordance with their royal priesthood, they inevitably face opposition from spiritual forces that seek to undermine their faith, hinder their mission, and disrupt their relationship with God. Overcoming these challenges requires reliance on God's strength, equipping oneself with the armor of God, and maintaining a posture of spiritual vigilance. In this chapter, we will explore the nature of spiritual battles, how believers can be equipped to face them, and the responsibility of standing firm in the power of God.

The Reality of Spiritual Warfare

From the moment a believer commits to living as part of the royal priesthood, they become engaged in spiritual warfare. The Bible makes it clear that the Christian life is not just a physical or intellectual journey; it is also a spiritual battle against unseen forces. Ephesians 6:12 describes this conflict: "For our struggle is not against flesh and blood, but against the rulers, against the authorities, against the powers of this dark world and against the spiritual forces of evil in the heavenly realms." This verse highlights that spiritual battles are fought in the heavenly realms and involve a clash between the kingdom of God and the kingdom of darkness.

The enemy, Satan, is described as a deceiver, accuser, and adversary who actively works to oppose God's people. 1 Peter 5:8 warns, "Be alert and of sober mind. Your enemy the devil prowls around like a roaring lion looking for someone to devour." Satan's goal is to disrupt the work of the royal priesthood by sowing seeds of doubt, fear, and division, and by tempting believers to sin or give up on their mission.

These spiritual battles can manifest in various forms, including:

1. Temptation to Sin: One of the most common ways the enemy attacks is through temptation. Just as Satan tempted Jesus in the wilderness (Matthew 4:1-11), he tempts

believers with sin, seeking to draw them away from God's will. These temptations may come in the form of pride, lust, greed, anger, or other sins that threaten to undermine a believer's witness and effectiveness in their priestly role.

2. Discouragement and Doubt: The enemy often seeks to discourage believers, making them doubt their calling, their worth, or God's faithfulness. John 8:44 describes Satan as the "father of lies," and he uses lies to make believers question God's promises, their identity in Christ, or the power of the gospel. Spiritual battles often involve overcoming thoughts of discouragement and doubt that aim to weaken a believer's resolve.

3. Opposition and Persecution: Throughout history, believers have faced opposition and persecution for their faith. 2 Timothy 3:12 warns, "In fact, everyone who wants to live a godly life in Christ Jesus will be persecuted." While this may come in the form of societal rejection, discrimination, or even physical harm, it is part of the spiritual battle that believers must be prepared to endure.

4. Distraction and Complacency: One of the subtle tactics of the enemy is to distract believers from their mission and make them complacent. By filling their lives with busyness, entertainment, or worldly pursuits, Satan seeks to divert attention from the things of God. 1 John 2:16 cautions

against the "lust of the flesh, the lust of the eyes, and the pride of life," which can pull believers away from their focus on God's kingdom.

Equipping with the Armor of God

To overcome these spiritual battles, believers must be equipped with the tools that God has provided. Ephesians 6:10-18 outlines the armor of God, which is essential for standing firm in the face of spiritual opposition. This armor enables believers to rely on God's strength rather than their own, recognizing that the battle belongs to the Lord (1 Samuel 17:47).

1. The Belt of Truth: Truth is the foundation of the believer's defense against deception and lies. The belt of truth represents the believer's commitment to living in the truth of God's Word and rejecting the lies of the enemy. John 8:32 says, "Then you will know the truth, and the truth will set you free." Believers must be grounded in Scripture, using it as a lens through which they interpret their experiences and decisions.

2. The Breastplate of Righteousness: The breastplate of righteousness symbolizes the righteousness that believers have in Christ. It protects the heart, which is the seat of emotions and desires, from the attacks of guilt, shame, and condemnation. 2 Corinthians 5:21 reminds believers that

"God made Him who had no sin to be sin for us, so that in Him we might become the righteousness of God." Knowing that their righteousness comes from Christ allows believers to stand firm in their identity, even when the enemy accuses them.

3. The Gospel of Peace (Shoes): The shoes of the gospel of peace represent readiness and stability in the believer's walk with God. The gospel provides peace with God, and believers are called to spread that peace to others. Isaiah 52:7 says, "How beautiful on the mountains are the feet of those who bring good news." With this peace, believers can stand firm, even in difficult circumstances, knowing that God is in control.

4. The Shield of Faith: The shield of faith is essential for protecting against the "fiery darts" of the enemy—temptations, doubts, and attacks that threaten to shake the believer's confidence in God. Hebrews 11:1 defines faith as "confidence in what we hope for and assurance about what we do not see." By trusting in God's promises and faithfulness, believers can extinguish the lies and schemes of the enemy.

5. The Helmet of Salvation: The helmet of salvation guards the mind, reminding believers of the security and assurance they have in their salvation through Christ. 1

Thessalonians 5:8 speaks of "the hope of salvation as a helmet." By keeping their minds focused on the hope of eternal life, believers are able to resist the discouragement and confusion that the enemy seeks to plant in their thoughts.

6. The Sword of the Spirit: The sword of the Spirit is the Word of God, the only offensive weapon in the armor of God. Hebrews 4:12 describes the Word as "living and active, sharper than any double-edged sword." By speaking and applying Scripture, believers can cut through the lies of the enemy and claim the promises of God in their lives. Jesus modeled this during His temptation in the wilderness, using Scripture to refute Satan's lies (Matthew 4:1-11).

7. Praying in the Spirit: In addition to the armor, prayer is a crucial weapon in spiritual warfare. Ephesians 6:18 instructs believers to "pray in the Spirit on all occasions with all kinds of prayers and requests." Through prayer, believers stay connected to God, receive His guidance, and intercede on behalf of others. Prayer is both a defensive and offensive tool in the believer's spiritual arsenal, keeping them aligned with God's will and protected from the enemy's attacks.

Relying on God's Strength

While believers are called to engage in spiritual battles, they are never expected to fight in their own strength. Ephesians 6:10 emphasizes, "Be strong in the Lord and in His mighty power." This means that victory in spiritual warfare comes not from human effort or strategy but from reliance on God's power, which is made available to every believer through the Holy Spirit.

1. Strength in Weakness: One of the paradoxes of spiritual battles is that believers often experience God's strength most clearly in their moments of weakness. 2 Corinthians 12:9 records God's words to the apostle Paul: "My grace is sufficient for you, for my power is made perfect in weakness." Rather than relying on their own abilities, believers must learn to depend on God's grace and trust that He will empower them to overcome every challenge.

2. Victory Through Christ: The ultimate victory over sin, death, and Satan was won by Jesus on the cross. Colossians 2:15 declares, "And having disarmed the powers and authorities, He made a public spectacle of them, triumphing over them by the cross." As believers stand in the finished work of Christ, they can face spiritual battles with confidence, knowing that they are fighting from a place of victory, not for victory. Romans 8:37 reminds believers that "we are more than conquerors through Him who loved us."

3. The Guidance of the Holy Spirit: In the midst of spiritual battles, believers are not left to fight alone. The Holy Spirit provides guidance, wisdom, and strength. John 14:26

promises that the Holy Spirit will "teach you all things and will remind you of everything I have said to you." Through prayer and sensitivity to the Spirit's leading, believers can discern the enemy's tactics and respond with wisdom and power.

The Responsibility to Stand Firm

As part of their royal priesthood, believers have the responsibility to stand firm in the face of spiritual opposition. Ephesians 6:13 commands, "Therefore put on the full armor of God, so that when the

day of evil comes, you may be able to stand your ground, and after you have done everything, to stand." This call to stand firm is not passive; it requires active engagement in the spiritual battle, continually relying on God's strength, using the armor of God, and resisting the enemy's attacks.

1. Resisting the Devil: James 4:7 offers a simple but powerful strategy: "Submit yourselves, then, to God. Resist the devil, and he will flee from you." By submitting to God's will and resisting the temptations and lies of the enemy, believers can stand firm in their faith and experience victory. Resisting the devil may involve rejecting sinful thoughts, standing up for righteousness, or speaking the truth of Scripture over a situation.

2. Standing Together in Unity: Spiritual battles are not meant to be fought in isolation. As part of the body of Christ,

believers are called to support one another, pray for each other, and stand together in unity. Ecclesiastes 4:12 teaches, "Though one may be overpowered, two can defend themselves. A cord of three strands is not quickly broken." The church plays a vital role in encouraging and strengthening one another during times of spiritual attack, providing accountability, counsel, and prayer.

3. Persevering in the Face of Trials: Spiritual battles often require perseverance. James 1:12 encourages, "Blessed is the one who perseveres under trial because, having stood the test, that person will receive the crown of life that the Lord has promised to those who love Him." Standing firm in faith, even when the battle is long and difficult, brings spiritual growth and rewards. Believers are called to endure, trusting that God will bring them through every challenge and use these experiences to strengthen their faith.

Living as kings and priests involves engaging in spiritual battles and standing firm in the face of opposition. These challenges are inevitable but not insurmountable, as believers are equipped with the armor of God and empowered by the Holy Spirit. By relying on God's strength, applying His Word, and standing together in unity, the royal priesthood can overcome every attack of the enemy and continue to fulfill their calling.

In the next chapter, we will explore how believers can cultivate deeper spiritual authority and grow in their effectiveness as representatives of God's kingdom on earth, continuing to live out their identity as kings and priests with boldness and faith.

Maintaining Holiness

As part of the royal priesthood, maintaining holiness is both a privilege and a continuous responsibility for every believer. Holiness reflects God's character and calls believers to live lives that are set apart, pure, and obedient to His will. While the pursuit of holiness is a lifelong journey, it is essential for fulfilling the role of a priest in God's kingdom. Maintaining holiness requires vigilance against sin, regularly seeking God's forgiveness, and striving to live in obedience and purity before Him. In this chapter, we will explore the importance of holiness, the process of sanctification, and practical steps believers can take to remain holy in a world full of temptations.

The Call to Holiness

Holiness is at the core of the believer's identity as part of the royal priesthood. 1 Peter 1:15-16 emphasizes this calling: "But just as He who called you is holy, so be holy in all you do; for it is written: 'Be holy, because I am holy.'" This call is rooted in God's very nature—He is holy, and as His people, believers are called to reflect that holiness in their lives.

Holiness means being set apart for God's purposes, living in a way that reflects His character, and rejecting the influences of sin and worldliness. It is not merely about following a set of rules but about having a heart and mind transformed by the Holy Spirit to align with God's will. Romans 12:1-2 describes this transformation: "Do not conform to the pattern of this world, but be transformed by the renewing of your mind. Then you will be able to test and approve what God's will is—His good, pleasing and perfect will."

Holiness is both a positional reality and a practical pursuit. Positionally, believers are made holy by the work of Jesus Christ on the cross; through His sacrifice, they are declared righteous before God (2 Corinthians 5:21). Practically, however, believers must actively pursue holiness in their daily lives by choosing to walk in obedience to God's commands and resisting the temptation to sin.

Vigilance Against Sin

While believers are declared holy in Christ, the reality of living in a fallen world means that they must remain vigilant against sin. The Bible describes the Christian life as a battle between the desires of the flesh and the guidance of the Holy Spirit. Galatians 5:17 explains, "For the flesh desires what is contrary to the Spirit, and the Spirit what is contrary to the flesh. They are in conflict with each other, so that you are not to do whatever you want."

Vigilance against sin requires an awareness of the enemy's tactics and a commitment to guarding one's heart, mind, and actions. 1 Peter 5:8 warns believers, "Be alert and of sober mind. Your enemy the devil prowls around like a roaring lion looking for someone to devour." Satan seeks to lead believers away from God through temptation, deception, and distraction. Therefore, it is crucial for believers to remain spiritually alert and rooted in the truth of God's Word.

Practical ways to stay vigilant against sin include:

1. Guarding the Mind and Heart: The mind and heart are often the battlegrounds where sin takes root. Proverbs 4:23 advises, "Above all else, guard your heart, for everything you do flows from it." Believers must be careful about what they allow to influence their thoughts and desires, avoiding exposure to media, conversations, or environments that could lead them into temptation. Philippians 4:8 offers a positive framework for this: "Whatever is true, whatever is noble, whatever is right, whatever is pure, whatever is lovely,

whatever is admirable—if anything is excellent or praiseworthy—think about such things."

2. Avoiding Temptation: Vigilance also means actively avoiding situations that may lead to sin. 1 Corinthians 10:13 reminds believers that "No temptation has overtaken you except what is common to mankind. And God is faithful; He will not let you be tempted beyond what you can bear." While temptation is inevitable, believers can take steps to minimize its power by staying away from environments, relationships, or habits that make them more susceptible to sin.

3. Accountability and Fellowship: Maintaining holiness is not something believers are meant to do alone. Being part of a community of faith provides accountability and support in the pursuit of holiness. Hebrews 10:24-25 encourages believers to "consider how we may spur one another on toward love and good deeds, not giving up meeting together." Trusted Christian friends and mentors can help keep one another accountable, offering encouragement, prayer, and guidance in moments of weakness.

Seeking God's Forgiveness

Despite their best efforts, believers will still face moments when they fall into sin. When this happens, it is essential to respond by seeking God's forgiveness and trusting in His grace. The Bible reassures believers that when they confess their sins, God is faithful to forgive and restore them to a right relationship with Him. 1 John 1:9 promises, "If we confess our sins, He is faithful and just and will forgive us our sins and purify us from all unrighteousness."

Seeking forgiveness is not just a one-time event; it is part of the ongoing process of sanctification. Sanctification is the work of the Holy Spirit in the believer's life, transforming them into the image of Christ over time. While justification—being made right with God—is a one-time event, sanctification is a continual process of growth and renewal.

The process of seeking God's forgiveness involves:

1. Confession: Confession is the acknowledgment of sin before God. Psalm 32:5 demonstrates the importance of confession: "Then I acknowledged my sin to You and did not cover up my iniquity. I said, 'I will confess my transgressions to the Lord.' And You forgave the guilt of my sin." Confession requires humility and a willingness to be honest about one's failures, trusting that God's grace is sufficient to cover all sins.

2. Repentance: True repentance goes beyond confession; it involves a change of heart and a commitment to turn away from sin. Acts 3:19 calls believers to "Repent, then, and turn to God, so that your sins may be wiped out, that times of refreshing may come from the Lord."

Repentance is not just about feeling sorry for sin but about choosing to realign one's life with God's will and pursuing holiness with renewed determination.

3. Restoration and Renewal: After seeking forgiveness, believers can experience the joy of restoration and the renewal of their relationship with God. Psalm 51:10 is a prayer for this kind of renewal: "Create in me a pure heart, O God, and renew a steadfast spirit within me." God's grace not only forgives sin but also empowers believers to move forward in holiness, trusting in His strength to overcome future temptations.

Striving for Purity and Obedience

The pursuit of holiness involves an ongoing commitment to live in purity and obedience to God's Word. 2 Corinthians 7:1 encourages believers, "Since we have these promises, dear friends, let us purify ourselves from everything that contaminates body and spirit, perfecting holiness out of reverence for God." Holiness is both an inward transformation and an outward expression of a life that is fully devoted to God.

1. Obedience to God's Word: Maintaining holiness requires a commitment to obeying God's commands as revealed in Scripture. John 14:15 reminds believers, "If you love Me, keep My commands." Obedience is not legalism; it

is an expression of love and reverence for God. Believers demonstrate their desire to maintain holiness by aligning their lives with the teachings of the Bible, seeking to live according to God's standards rather than the world's.

2. Fleeing from Sin: In addition to obeying God's Word, maintaining holiness involves actively fleeing from sin. 2 Timothy 2:22 instructs, "Flee the evil desires of youth and pursue righteousness, faith, love, and peace, along with those who call on the Lord out of a pure heart." Pursuing holiness requires intentionality—choosing to reject sinful behaviors and pursue what is righteous, pure, and honoring to God.

3. Relying on the Holy Spirit: The pursuit of holiness is not something believers can achieve in their own strength. It is only through the power of the Holy Spirit that believers can resist sin and grow in purity. Galatians 5:16 teaches, "So I say, walk by the Spirit, and you will not gratify the desires of the flesh." The Holy Spirit empowers believers to overcome temptation, convict them of sin, and guide them into greater holiness. By staying connected to the Spirit through prayer and obedience, believers can continually grow in purity and righteousness.

4. Living as a Witness: Holiness is not only for personal benefit; it is also a powerful witness to the world. Matthew 5:16 encourages believers to "let your light shine

before others, that they may see your good deeds and glorify your Father in heaven." When believers live lives of purity and obedience, they reflect God's holiness to those around them, drawing others to the truth and grace of the gospel.

Maintaining holiness is a continuous pursuit that requires vigilance, reliance on God's grace, and a commitment to live in purity and obedience. As members of the royal priesthood, believers are called to reflect God's holiness in their daily lives, staying alert to the dangers of sin, seeking forgiveness when they fall, and striving to walk in righteousness. This pursuit is not easy, but it is essential for fulfilling the believer's role as a representative of God's kingdom.

Fulfilling the Great Commission

The Great Commission is at the heart of the calling and responsibility of the royal priesthood. Jesus' final command to His disciples, recorded in Matthew 28:19-20, serves as the foundation for the mission of every believer: "Therefore go and make disciples of all nations, baptizing them in the name of the Father and of the Son and of the Holy Spirit, and teaching them to obey everything I have commanded you. And surely I am with you always, to the very end of the age." This commission charges believers with the task of sharing the gospel, making disciples, and teaching others to obey Christ's commands. In this chapter, we will explore how believers can practically fulfill this mission, the challenges they may face, and the importance of relying on Christ's authority and presence in the process.

The Core Responsibility of the Royal Priesthood

As part of the royal priesthood, every believer is given the responsibility of fulfilling the Great Commission. While some may view the work of evangelism, discipleship, and teaching as tasks reserved for pastors or missionaries, the Great Commission makes it clear that these responsibilities are for all who follow Christ. Every member of the royal priesthood is called to represent Christ in the world and to actively participate in the mission of bringing others into a relationship with Him.

1. Sharing the Gospel: The first part of the Great Commission involves sharing the gospel—the good news of salvation through Jesus Christ. Romans 1:16 declares, "For I am not ashamed of the gospel, because it is the power of God that brings salvation to everyone who believes." The gospel message is the core truth that transforms lives, and believers are entrusted with the privilege of sharing this message with others.

Sharing the gospel can happen in a variety of ways, from personal conversations with friends and family to public declarations of faith. 1 Peter 3:15 encourages believers to always be ready to share their faith: "Always be prepared to give an answer to everyone who asks you to give the reason for the hope that you have." This readiness means being open to opportunities for evangelism in everyday life, whether at work, in the community, or even online.

2. Making Disciples: The second part of the Great Commission is making disciples. This goes beyond evangelism and involves helping people grow in their relationship with Christ. Matthew 28:19 calls believers not just to share the gospel, but to "make disciples of all nations." Discipleship is about walking alongside new believers, teaching them the foundational truths of the faith, and helping them mature in their spiritual journey.

Making disciples is an ongoing process that involves teaching, mentoring, and modeling a life of obedience to Christ. 2 Timothy 2:2 captures the essence of discipleship: "And the things you have heard me say in the presence of many witnesses entrust to reliable people who will also be qualified to teach others." Discipleship is meant to be multiplicative—as believers are discipled, they, in turn, disciple others, continuing the work of the Great Commission across generations.

3. Teaching Obedience to Christ's Commands: The Great Commission also includes the instruction to "teach them to obey everything I have commanded you" (Matthew 28:20). Teaching others to obey Christ's commands is an essential part of helping believers grow in holiness and spiritual maturity. John 14:15 emphasizes the importance of obedience: "If you love me, keep my commands." As disciples of Jesus, believers are called to teach and encourage one another to live in accordance with God's Word.

This teaching is not just about head knowledge; it is about cultivating obedient hearts that seek to follow Christ in all areas of life. Through Bible study, sermons, discipleship groups, and personal mentoring, believers can pass on the truths of Scripture and help others apply them in practical ways.

Overcoming Challenges in Fulfilling the Great Commission

Fulfilling the Great Commission comes with significant challenges. As believers engage in evangelism, discipleship, and teaching, they will encounter spiritual resistance, cultural barriers, and personal limitations.

However, these challenges can be overcome through reliance on God's power, wisdom, and guidance.

1. Spiritual Resistance: The work of fulfilling the Great Commission is ultimately a spiritual battle. 2 Corinthians 4:4 explains that "the god of this age has blinded the minds of unbelievers, so that they cannot see the light of the gospel that displays the glory of Christ." Satan actively works to prevent people from hearing and receiving the gospel, and believers may encounter resistance in the form of apathy, hostility, or misunderstanding.

Overcoming spiritual resistance requires persistent prayer and dependence on the Holy Spirit. Ephesians 6:18 encourages believers to "pray in the Spirit on all occasions with all kinds of prayers and requests." By covering evangelistic and discipleship efforts in prayer, believers invite the Holy Spirit to soften hearts, open minds, and break down spiritual strongholds that hinder people from accepting the truth.

2. Cultural Barriers: Sharing the gospel and making disciples in a diverse world often means navigating cultural differences, language barriers, and varying worldviews. 1 Corinthians 9:22 captures Paul's approach to overcoming these barriers: "I have become all things to all people so that by all possible means I might save some." Paul was willing to

adapt his approach to the cultural context of his audience without compromising the gospel message.

Believers today must likewise be culturally sensitive as they seek to fulfill the Great Commission. This may involve learning about the beliefs and practices of different cultures, finding ways to communicate the gospel in a way that resonates with people's experiences, and building relationships of trust and respect. The goal is to present the unchanging truth of the gospel in ways that are understandable and relevant to people from all walks of life.

3. Personal Limitations: Many believers feel inadequate or ill-equipped to share the gospel, make disciples, or teach others. They may feel they lack the necessary knowledge, confidence, or skills to fulfill the Great Commission. However, Jesus' promise in the Great Commission is that He will always be with His followers as they carry out this mission: "And surely I am with you always, to the very end of the age" (Matthew 28:20).

Believers can take comfort in knowing that it is not their own abilities that will bring people to Christ but the power of the Holy Spirit working through them. Acts 1:8 promises, "But you will receive power when the Holy Spirit comes on you; and you will be My witnesses in Jerusalem, and in all Judea and Samaria, and to the ends of the earth." By relying on the Spirit's power and seeking opportunities to grow in their knowledge and skills, believers can overcome their personal limitations and be effective witnesses for Christ.

The Authority and Presence of Christ

A key element of the Great Commission is the authority and presence of Christ. Before giving His disciples the command to go and make disciples, Jesus declares, "All authority in heaven and on earth has been given to Me" (Matthew 28:18). This authority is foundational for the church's mission. Believers do not go in their own strength or authority; they go as representatives of the risen King, who has conquered sin, death, and the powers of darkness.

1. Authority in Evangelism and Discipleship: Jesus' authority gives believers the confidence to share the gospel and make disciples, knowing that He has the power to transform lives. Philippians 2:10-11 affirms that "at the name of Jesus every knee should bow, in heaven and on earth and under the earth, and every tongue acknowledge that Jesus Christ is Lord." As believers go out to fulfill the Great Commission, they do so under the authority of Christ, who has already secured the victory.

2. The Promise of His Presence: Jesus' promise to be with His followers "to the very end of the age" is a source of

comfort and strength as believers face the challenges of fulfilling the Great Commission. John 14:16-17 reassures believers that the Holy Spirit will dwell within them, empowering them for the work of the kingdom. The presence of Christ, through the Holy Spirit, enables believers to persevere in difficult circumstances, remain faithful in the face of opposition, and experience God's guidance as they share the gospel and disciple others.

Practical Ways to Fulfill the Great Commission

Fulfilling the Great Commission is not just for full-time missionaries or church leaders; it is a responsibility that all believers share. There are many practical ways in which the royal priesthood can engage in this mission on a daily basis:

1. Personal Evangelism: Sharing the gospel can start with personal relationships—family, friends, coworkers, and neighbors. Believers can look for natural opportunities to share their faith, whether through casual conversations, acts of kindness, or invitations to church or Bible study. Colossians 4:5-6 encourages believers to "be wise in the way you act toward outsiders; make the most of every opportunity. Let your conversation be always full of grace, seasoned with salt."

2. Mentoring and Discipleship: Every believer can be involved in discipling others, whether through one-on-one

mentoring, leading a small group, or participating in a discipleship class. Discipleship is about building relationships, sharing life, and helping others grow in their faith.

Proverbs 27:17 says, "As iron sharpens iron, so one person sharpens another." By investing in the spiritual growth of others, believers fulfill the Great Commission in a personal and meaningful way.

3. Serving in the Church: There are countless opportunities within the local church to support the mission of making disciples. Whether through teaching, serving in children's ministry, leading worship, or participating in outreach events, believers can use their gifts and talents to help others come to know Christ and grow in their faith. 1 Peter 4:10 encourages believers to "use whatever gift you have received to serve others, as faithful stewards of God's grace in its various forms."

4. Supporting Global Missions: While not all believers are called to serve as missionaries, they can still support global missions through prayer, financial giving, and advocacy. Romans 10:15 asks, "How can anyone preach unless they are sent?" By partnering with missionaries and organizations that are spreading the gospel around the world, believers play a vital role in fulfilling the Great Commission globally.

Fulfilling the Great Commission is one of the core responsibilities of the royal priesthood. Every believer is called to share the gospel, make disciples, and teach others to obey Christ's commands. While this mission comes with challenges, it is ultimately grounded in the authority and presence of Jesus, who empowers His followers to carry out His work on earth. By engaging in personal evangelism, discipleship, service in the church, and support for global missions, believers can actively participate in the Great Commission and continue the work of expanding God's kingdom.

CHAPTER 10

THE ETERNAL KINGDOM

The Future Reign with Christ

The calling of the royal priesthood extends far beyond this life, carrying into the promise of eternity. Believers are destined not only to serve God in the present world but also to reign with Christ in the new heaven and new earth, where they will experience perfect fellowship with God, reflect His glory, and fulfill their eternal roles as kings and priests. This chapter explores the biblical promise of the eternal kingdom, the role believers will play in the future reign with Christ, and the profound significance of living in anticipation of this glorious future.

The New Heaven and New Earth

The ultimate destiny of believers is described in Revelation 21:1-3, where John sees a vision of the new heaven and new earth: "Then I saw 'a new heaven and a new earth,' for the first heaven and the first earth had passed away, and there was no longer any sea. I saw the Holy City, the new Jerusalem, coming down out of heaven from God, prepared as a bride beautifully dressed for her husband. And I heard a loud voice from the throne saying, 'Look! God's dwelling place is now among the people, and He will dwell with them. They will be His people, and God Himself will be with them and be their God.'"

This passage reveals that the new heaven and new earth will be a place where believers experience perfect fellowship with God, free from the corruption and pain of the current world. In this new creation, the barriers between heaven and earth will be removed, and God's eternal kingdom will be fully established. Believers will dwell in the New Jerusalem, a city representing God's ultimate presence and the fulfillment of His promise to dwell among His people.

Key characteristics of the new heaven and new earth include:

1. Perfect Fellowship with God: God's promise to "dwell with" His people will be fully realized in the new heaven and new earth. This perfect fellowship with God, described as His dwelling place being among His people, will restore what was lost in Eden. Believers will no longer experience separation from God due to sin. Revelation 21:4

says, "He will wipe every tear from their eyes. There will be no more death or mourning or crying or pain, for the old order of things has passed away." This eternal relationship with God will bring joy, peace, and the fulfillment of every longing.

2. The Absence of Sin and Suffering: In the new heaven and new earth, the effects of sin—pain, suffering, and death—will no longer exist. The old order, tainted by the fall of humanity, will pass away, and believers will experience life in the fullness of God's holiness. Isaiah 65:17 echoes this vision: "See, I will create new heavens and a new earth. The former things will not be remembered, nor will they come to mind." The perfect holiness of God will saturate the new creation, and believers will dwell in purity and righteousness for eternity.

3. God's Glory Reflected in Creation: The new heaven and new earth will be filled with the glory of God. Revelation 21:23 says, "The city does not need the sun or the moon to shine on it, for the glory of God gives it light, and the Lamb is its lamp." This indicates that God's radiant presence will illuminate the entire creation, and believers will live in the full light of His glory. As part of the royal priesthood, believers will reflect God's glory as they serve Him and reign with Him.

The Role of Believers in the Eternal Kingdom

Believers will play a crucial role in the eternal kingdom as kings and priests, continuing to fulfill the call that began in this present life. Revelation 22:5 reveals the future role of believers: "There will be no more night. They will not need the light of a lamp or the light of the sun, for the Lord God will give them light. And they will reign for ever and ever."

1. Reigning with Christ: As kings, believers will reign with Christ in the new creation. This is the ultimate fulfillment of the calling to dominion that was given to humanity in Genesis 1:26, where God commanded mankind to rule over the earth. In the new heaven and new earth, this dominion will be restored, but it will no longer be marred by sin or rebellion. Believers will reign in perfect harmony with God's will, exercising authority as stewards of His creation. This reign will not be about power or control as understood in worldly terms but about serving and reflecting God's goodness and justice in all things.

2. Serving as Priests: As priests, believers will continue to serve God, offering worship and reflecting His holiness. The priestly role in the eternal kingdom involves not only worship but also intercession and service to God. Revelation 7:15 speaks of this eternal service: "Therefore, they are before the throne of God and serve Him day and night in His temple." In the new creation, the temple is God Himself, and

believers will serve Him directly, offering their lives as a continual act of worship. This service will be a joyful, fulfilling expression of love and gratitude for God's eternal grace.

3. Reflecting God's Glory: The eternal kingdom will be characterized by the radiant glory of God, and believers will reflect this glory as they serve and reign with Him. 2 Corinthians 3:18 gives a foretaste of this transformation: "And we all, who with unveiled faces contemplate the Lord's glory, are being transformed into His image with ever-increasing glory, which comes from the Lord, who is the Spirit." In the new creation, this transformation will be complete, and believers will fully reflect the glory of God in their resurrected bodies and holy lives.

Living in Anticipation of the Eternal Kingdom

While the promise of the new heaven and new earth is a future reality, it has profound implications for how believers live today. The anticipation of reigning with Christ in eternity should inspire believers to live in holiness, faithfulness, and mission, aligning their lives with God's eternal purposes.

1. Pursuing Holiness: Knowing that believers are destined to serve and reign in a kingdom where God's holiness is fully manifested should motivate them to pursue holiness in their daily lives. 1 Peter 1:14-16 encourages

believers, "As obedient children, do not conform to the evil desires you had when you lived in ignorance. But just as He who called you is holy, so be holy in all you do." Living in anticipation of the eternal kingdom involves striving to reflect God's holiness now, preparing to live in His presence forever.

2. Faithfulness in Service: The knowledge that believers will serve God eternally as priests should encourage them to be faithful in their service here on earth. 1 Corinthians 15:58 reminds believers, "Always give yourselves fully to the work of the Lord, because you know that your labor in the Lord is not in vain." Whether through acts of worship, ministry, or acts of kindness, believers are called to serve God with dedication, knowing that their service has eternal significance.

3. Living on Mission: The Great Commission (Matthew 28:19-20) and the hope of the eternal kingdom are deeply intertwined. As believers look forward to reigning with Christ, they are also called to invite others into this eternal reality by sharing the gospel and making disciples. 2 Peter 3:13-14 urges believers to live in light of the coming kingdom: "But in keeping with His promise we are looking forward to a new heaven and a new earth, where righteousness dwells. So then, dear friends, since you are looking forward to this, make every effort to be found spotless, blameless, and at peace with

Him." Evangelism and discipleship are essential aspects of preparing for the eternal reign with Christ.

4. Enduring Suffering and Trials: The hope of the eternal kingdom also gives believers the strength to endure suffering and trials in this life. Romans 8:18 offers perspective: "I consider that our present sufferings are not worth comparing with the glory that will be revealed in us." Knowing that eternal glory awaits, believers can persevere through difficulties, confident that their future with Christ far outweighs the temporary challenges of this world.

The promise of reigning with Christ in the new heaven and new earth is a glorious hope for every believer. As members of the royal priesthood, believers are called not only to serve and reign with Christ in this present life but also in eternity, where they will experience perfect fellowship with God, serve Him in holiness, and reflect His glory forever. This eternal reality should shape how believers live today, motivating them to pursue holiness, remain faithful in service, live on mission, and endure trials with hope.

The anticipation of the eternal kingdom is not merely a distant hope; it is a living reality that transforms the way believers engage with the world. As they look forward to the day when they will reign with Christ, they are empowered to live as faithful kings and priests in the here and now, advancing God's kingdom on earth as they prepare for its full manifestation in eternity.

The New Heaven and New Earth

A Restored Creation

The Bible paints a powerful and hopeful picture of a restored creation, where God's people will dwell with Him forever in the new heaven and new earth. This promise, found in both the Old and New Testaments, speaks of an eternal kingdom characterized by peace, righteousness, and the fullness of God's presence. The new heaven and new earth represent the culmination of God's redemptive plan, where the effects of sin, death, and suffering are completely eradicated, and all things are made new. In this chapter, we will explore the biblical promises concerning this future reality, the characteristics of the eternal kingdom, and the profound implications for believers today.

The Biblical Promise of a New Heaven and New Earth

The concept of a new heaven and new earth is introduced in the Old Testament and fulfilled in the New Testament. The prophet Isaiah foretold this future reality, saying, "See, I will create new heavens and a new earth. The former things will not be remembered, nor will they come to mind" (Isaiah 65:17). This prophecy reveals God's intention to completely renew and restore His creation, a theme that is echoed throughout Scripture.

In the New Testament, the apostle John's vision in the book of Revelation provides the clearest description of the new heaven and new earth. Revelation 21:1-3 declares, "Then I saw 'a new heaven and a new earth,' for the first heaven and the first earth had passed away, and there was no longer any sea. I saw the Holy City, the new Jerusalem, coming down out of heaven from God, prepared as a bride beautifully dressed for her husband. And I heard a loud voice from the throne saying, 'Look! God's dwelling place is now among the people, and He will dwell with them. They will be His people, and God Himself will be with them and be their God.'"

This passage reveals several key elements of the eternal kingdom:

1. The Passing Away of the Old: The new heaven and new earth replace the current, broken creation. Revelation 21:1 notes that the first heaven and earth will pass away, signifying the end of the present world as we know it. This transformation marks the final removal of all that is tainted by sin and corruption, making way for a new creation that is perfect and eternal.

2. The Holy City, New Jerusalem: The New Jerusalem is the dwelling place of God and His people. It is described as a city prepared like a bride for her husband, symbolizing the beauty, purity, and intimate relationship between God and His people. The New Jerusalem is the ultimate fulfillment of God's promise to dwell among His people (Leviticus 26:11-12), and in this city, the redeemed will live in perfect fellowship with God forever.

3. God's Presence with His People: One of the most remarkable aspects of the new heaven and new earth is the fullness of God's presence. In this restored creation, there is no longer any separation between God and humanity. God Himself will dwell with His people, fulfilling His desire for intimate fellowship. Revelation 21:3 states, "They will be His people, and God Himself will be with them and be their God." This perfect communion with God is the ultimate goal of redemption and the source of eternal joy for believers.

Characteristics of the Eternal Kingdom

The new heaven and new earth are characterized by a number of profound and transformative realities that distinguish them from the present world. In this eternal kingdom, believers will experience a life that is defined by peace, righteousness, and the unending presence of God.

1. Peace: In the new creation, the peace of God will permeate every aspect of life. The Hebrew word for peace, shalom, encompasses not only the absence of conflict but also the presence of wholeness, harmony, and well-being. This peace will characterize the eternal kingdom, where there will be no more strife, suffering, or division. Isaiah 65:25 gives a picture of this peace: "The wolf and the lamb will feed together, and the lion will eat straw like the ox." In the new heaven and new earth, all of creation will exist in perfect harmony, reflecting the peace that comes from God's rule.

2. Righteousness: The eternal kingdom is a place where righteousness reigns. 2 Peter 3:13 promises, "But in keeping with His promise we are looking forward to a new heaven and a new earth, where righteousness dwells." In this new creation, sin will no longer have any power or influence. Believers will live in perfect righteousness, free from the corruption of sin, and in full alignment with God's will. This righteousness will be expressed not only in the moral purity of God's people but also in the justice and fairness that will characterize every aspect of life in the eternal kingdom.

3. The Fullness of God's Presence: The most defining characteristic of the new heaven and new earth is the unhindered presence of God. In the eternal kingdom, God's glory will fill the entire creation, and His presence will be the

light that illuminates everything. Revelation 21:23 says, "The city does not need the sun or the moon to shine on it, for the glory of God gives it light, and the Lamb is its lamp." This glory will not be distant or veiled but will be fully revealed to those who dwell in the new creation. Believers will live in the immediate presence of God, experiencing the fullness of His love, grace, and power for all eternity.

4. No More Suffering, Death, or Sin: One of the most comforting promises of the new heaven and new earth is the end of suffering and death. Revelation 21:4 declares, "He will wipe every tear from their eyes. There will be no more death or mourning or crying or pain, for the old order of things has passed away." In this eternal kingdom, the effects of sin will be completely erased. There will be no more sickness, sorrow, or loss. The promise of eternal life with Christ means that believers will experience an existence free from the pain and brokenness of the current world, living forever in joy and peace.

The Role of Believers in the New Heaven and New Earth

In the new heaven and new earth, believers will continue their roles as kings and priests, serving and reigning with Christ. This eternal calling will be the fulfillment of the royal priesthood that began in this life, as believers live in perfect harmony with God's will and purpose.

1. Reigning with Christ: As kings, believers will share in Christ's reign over the new creation. Revelation 22:5 promises, "And they will reign for ever and ever." This reign is not about power or domination in the earthly sense but about sharing in Christ's authority and fulfilling God's purposes for His creation. Believers will exercise stewardship over the new creation, reflecting God's justice, love, and wisdom as they serve alongside Christ.

2. Serving as Priests: As priests, believers will offer continual worship and service to God in the new creation. Revelation 7:15 describes this eternal priestly role: "Therefore, they are before the throne of God and serve Him day and night in His temple." The eternal kingdom will be marked by unceasing worship, where believers experience the joy of serving God directly in His presence. This priestly service will be an expression of love, gratitude, and reverence for God's eternal grace and goodness.

3. Reflecting God's Glory: In the new heaven and new earth, believers will fully reflect the glory of God. 2 Corinthians 3:18 speaks of this transformation: "And we all, who with unveiled faces contemplate the Lord's glory, are being transformed into His image with ever-increasing glory,

which comes from the Lord, who is the Spirit." In the eternal kingdom, this transformation will be complete, and believers will radiate the glory of God in their resurrected bodies, perfectly reflecting His image and character.

Living in Anticipation of the New Heaven and New Earth

The promise of the new heaven and new earth has profound implications for how believers live today. Knowing that this eternal kingdom awaits should inspire believers to live with hope, purpose, and a sense of mission.

1. Living with Hope: The future reality of the new heaven and new earth gives believers hope in the midst of life's challenges and trials. Romans 8:18 reminds us, "I consider that our present sufferings are not worth comparing with the glory that will be revealed in us." This hope enables believers to endure suffering with the knowledge that an eternal glory awaits them in God's presence.

2. Pursuing Holiness and Righteousness: The promise of a future kingdom where righteousness dwells should motivate believers to pursue holiness in their daily lives. 2 Peter 3:11-12 exhorts, "Since everything will be destroyed in this way, what kind of people ought you to be? You ought to live holy and godly lives as you look forward to the day of God." Living in anticipation of the new heaven and new earth

means striving to reflect God's character now, aligning our lives with His will and purpose.

The New Heaven and New Earth

Engaging in the Mission of God

The promise of the eternal kingdom fuels the church's mission to share the gospel and make disciples, knowing that this new heaven and new earth is the ultimate destination for God's people. 2 Peter 3:13-14 says, "But in keeping with His promise we are looking forward to a new heaven and a new earth, where righteousness dwells. So then, dear friends, since you are looking forward to this, make every effort to be found spotless, blameless, and at peace with Him." This future reality should inspire believers to actively participate in God's mission on earth, helping others come to know Christ and enter into the eternal kingdom.

The anticipation of the new creation motivates believers to:

1. Preach the Gospel: The message of the gospel is the means by which people can enter the new heaven and new earth. Jesus commanded His followers to go into all the world and proclaim the good news of salvation (Matthew 28:19-20). In light of eternity, preaching the gospel becomes even more urgent, as it invites others to partake in the life that God has

prepared for those who love Him. Romans 10:14-15 asks, "How can they hear without someone preaching to them?" Sharing the gospel is essential in pointing people to Christ, the only way to salvation and eternal life in the kingdom of God.

2. Make Disciples: Engaging in the mission of making disciples is about helping others grow in their faith and preparing them for their eternal calling. Jesus' command in the Great Commission is not just to make converts but to "teach them to obey everything I have commanded you" (Matthew 28:20). Discipleship involves walking alongside others as they learn to follow Christ, helping them understand their role in God's kingdom, and preparing them for the eternal reign with Christ. By investing in the spiritual growth of others, believers are expanding the reach of God's kingdom.

3. Advance God's Kingdom: The church is called to actively advance God's kingdom in the world, reflecting the values and priorities of the coming new creation. This includes advocating for justice, caring for the vulnerable, and promoting peace—all of which reflect the righteousness, peace, and wholeness that will characterize the new heaven and new earth. Micah 6:8 reminds believers to "act justly and to love mercy and to walk humbly with your God." By living out these values now, the church provides a foretaste of the

eternal kingdom and draws others to experience the fullness of life in Christ.

4. Live with Purpose and Urgency: Knowing that the present world will one day pass away and be replaced by a new creation should fill believers with a sense of purpose and urgency. The reality of eternity changes how believers approach their time, relationships, and resources. Ephesians 5:15-16 urges, "Be very careful, then, how you live—not as unwise but as wise, making the most of every opportunity, because the days are evil." Living in anticipation of the new heaven and new earth means living intentionally for God's kingdom, prioritizing what matters in light of eternity, and using every opportunity to serve God and others.

The promise of the new heaven and new earth is a glorious hope for every believer, pointing to a future where God's people will dwell with Him forever in a restored creation characterized by peace, righteousness, and the fullness of His presence. This eternal kingdom represents the culmination of God's redemptive plan, where sin, suffering, and death are no more, and believers reign with Christ in perfect harmony and joy.

As members of the royal priesthood, believers are called to live in anticipation of this future reality, reflecting the values of God's kingdom in their daily lives and engaging in

His mission to share the gospel and make disciples. This promise of eternity should inspire believers to live with hope, purpose, and urgency, knowing that their present efforts to advance God's kingdom have eternal significance.

Ultimately, the new heaven and new earth remind believers that the best is yet to come. As they wait for Christ's return and the full establishment of His kingdom, they are empowered to live faithfully, trusting in the God who is making all things new.

The unseen is eternal. The hope of eternity empowers believers to endure hardship with faith, knowing that their future is secure in Christ.

The eternal roles of kings and priests are the ultimate fulfillment of God's redemptive plan for believers. In the new heaven and new earth, believers will reign with Christ, exercising authority in perfect harmony with God's will, and they will serve as priests, offering eternal worship and living in the fullness of God's presence. This eternal calling is the culmination of everything believers are called to in this life, and it is the source of their eternal joy, purpose, and hope.

As believers look forward to the day when they will fully step into these roles, they are called to live in light of this eternal destiny now—embracing their current calling, living with an eternal perspective, and persevering with hope, knowing that their future is secure in the presence of their Savior and King.

Our Eternal Role as Kings and Priests

Persevering with Hope

Finally, the promise of reigning and serving with Christ in eternity gives believers the strength to persevere through difficulties, knowing that their present sufferings are temporary in light of the eternal glory that awaits them. 2 Corinthians 4:17-18 offers this encouragement: "For our light and momentary troubles are achieving for us an eternal glory that far outweighs them all. So we fix our eyes not on what is seen, but on what is unseen, since what is seen is temporary, but what is unseen is eternal." This eternal perspective helps believers endure trials with the knowledge that everything they experience in this life is preparing them for the greater glory they will share with Christ in the new heaven and new earth.

1. Enduring Trials with an Eternal Perspective: In the midst of hardships, believers are called to endure by fixing their eyes on what is unseen—the eternal kingdom and the promises of God. This eternal focus helps them to see beyond the challenges of the present moment, understanding that every trial and tribulation is working to produce a greater

good that they will one day fully realize in eternity. Romans 8:18 echoes this truth: "I consider that our present sufferings are not worth comparing with the glory that will be revealed in us." When believers maintain this perspective, they can persevere with hope, knowing that their struggles are not in vain.

2. Strength from God's Promises: The promise of eternal life and the roles of kings and priests offer strength and comfort in the face of life's difficulties. God's Word provides countless assurances of His faithfulness to bring believers through trials and into the fullness of His presence. James 1:12 encourages, "Blessed is the one who perseveres under trial because, having stood the test, that person will receive the crown of life that the Lord has promised to those who love Him." The crown of life and the promise of reigning with Christ remind believers that their endurance is part of their preparation for eternity.

3. Focusing on the Unseen: The temporary nature of earthly struggles becomes clear when compared to the eternal nature of the kingdom to come. While earthly trials can feel overwhelming, 2 Corinthians 4:18 teaches that what is seen is temporary, but what is unseen is eternal. This passage invites believers to shift their focus from the visible, fleeting difficulties of this world to the invisible, lasting promises of

God. As they do so, they gain the strength to press on, empowered by the knowledge that their eternal reward far outweighs their present challenges.

4. Encouragement in Community: Persevering through trials is not something believers are called to do alone. The community of faith plays a critical role in helping one another endure with hope. Hebrews 10:24-25 encourages believers to "consider how we may spur one another on toward love and good deeds, not giving up meeting together… but encouraging one another—and all the more as you see the Day approaching." As believers walk through difficulties, they can draw strength from their fellow brothers and sisters in Christ, encouraging one another with the truths of God's promises and supporting each other in prayer and fellowship.

Eternal Glory Awaits

The promise of reigning and serving with Christ in the new heaven and new earth provides the ultimate source of hope and motivation for believers as they navigate the challenges of this life. The knowledge that they will share in Christ's eternal kingdom, fulfilling their roles as kings and priests, gives them the strength to persevere, knowing that their present struggles are part of God's plan to prepare them for the glory that lies ahead.

In the face of trials, believers are called to fix their eyes on what is unseen—the eternal kingdom that is their true home. As they do so, they can endure with hope, confident that every challenge they face is temporary and that their eternal future with Christ is secure. The roles of kingship and priesthood that believers are called to in this life will be fully realized in the new creation, where they will reign with Christ and worship Him in His presence forever.

This glorious future shapes how believers live today—empowering them to embrace their current calling, to live with an eternal perspective, and to persevere with hope, all while looking forward to the day when they will enter into the fullness of God's eternal kingdom. "He who is seated on the throne said, 'I am making everything new!'" (Revelation 21:5)

CONCLUSION

Recap of Key Points

The identity and calling of believers as kings and priests is one of the most profound biblical truths, deeply rooted in Scripture and filled with far-reaching implications for both individual and corporate life. This truth reveals the unique role that God has entrusted to His people both now and in the age to come. As kings and priests, believers are called to reflect God's glory, serve His purposes, and carry out His will on earth and in the eternal kingdom.

Throughout this book, we explored several key aspects of this divine calling:

1. Biblical Foundation: We began by establishing the biblical foundation for the royal priesthood, beginning with God's promise to the Israelites in Exodus 19:6, where He declared them to be a kingdom of priests and a holy nation. This theme was further developed in the New Testament, particularly in 1 Peter 2:9, which extends this royal priesthood

to all who believe in Christ, calling them to declare the praises of God and live as representatives of His kingdom.

2. Kingship and Priesthood in Ancient Israel: We examined the roles of kings and priests in ancient Israel, highlighting how these offices served as earthly reflections of divine authority and mediation. Kings like David and Solomon were charged with governing the people in righteousness, while priests from the tribe of Levi interceded for the people and maintained Israel's covenant relationship with God. These roles ultimately point to the perfect kingship and priesthood of Christ.

3. Jesus Christ: The Ultimate King and Priest: At the heart of the royal priesthood is Jesus Christ, the perfect fulfillment of both kingship and priesthood. As the King of Kings, Christ rules over all creation with absolute authority, and as the High Priest, He has offered the ultimate sacrifice for sin, making a way for humanity to be reconciled to God. In Christ, believers are not only saved but are also brought into a new relationship with God as co-heirs with Christ, sharing in His royal and priestly roles.

4. The Church as a Royal Priesthood: We explored the corporate identity of the church as a royal priesthood, called to work together in unity to proclaim the gospel, make disciples, and serve the world in the name of Christ. The

church's mission is a reflection of its identity, as believers collectively advance God's kingdom by living out their calling in worship, service, and witness.

5. Living as Kings and Priests Today: We considered the practical implications of living as kings and priests in the present age. As kings, believers are called to exercise spiritual authority, stand against evil, and steward God's creation with wisdom and integrity. As priests, they are called to lives of holiness, intercession, and service, offering spiritual sacrifices of prayer, worship, and love.

6. The Eternal Kingdom and the Future Role of Believers: Finally, we looked forward to the eternal kingdom, where believers will fully realize their roles as kings and priests. In the new heaven and new earth, they will reign with Christ, serve in His presence, and worship Him without ceasing. This eternal role is the culmination of their earthly calling and the fulfillment of God's redemptive plan for all of creation.

A Profound Truth with Lasting Implications

The identity of believers as kings and priests is not just an abstract theological concept; it is a profound truth with lasting implications for how we live, serve, and worship both now and in eternity. It calls us to a life of purpose, as we participate in God's kingdom work here on earth, knowing that our efforts carry eternal significance.

This identity also calls us to live in hope, as we look forward to the day when we will reign with Christ in the new creation, where all things will be made new. As kings, we will exercise authority under Christ's rule, and as priests, we will offer eternal worship in His presence, reflecting His glory and love in a perfect, restored creation.

As we live in the light of this calling, may we continually grow in our understanding of what it means to be kings and priests in God's kingdom, faithfully serving Him with our lives and eagerly anticipating the fulfillment of His promises in eternity.

ENCOURAGEMENT FOR BELIEVERS

Believers are encouraged to fully embrace their identity as kings and priests, living out the profound calling that God has placed on their lives. This identity is not simply a title but a reflection of the immense privilege and responsibility that comes with being part of God's royal priesthood. As such, believers are invited to step into their roles with confidence, purpose, and hope, knowing that they are part of God's eternal plan.

Embrace Your Identity

As a king and priest in God's kingdom, you have been given a position of honor and influence. God has chosen you to reign with Christ and to serve Him both now and in the life to come. Embracing this identity means:

- Understanding your worth in Christ. You are not defined by the world's standards or by your past but by the new creation that you are in Him (2 Corinthians 5:17). You are chosen, loved, and set apart for God's purposes.

- Living with authority in Christ. As a king, you are called to stand firm against evil, exercise spiritual dominion, and advance God's kingdom on earth. You have been given authority through Christ to pray boldly, confront injustice, and live as a beacon of hope and righteousness.

- Serving as a priest to those around you. As a priest, you are called to intercede for others, offer spiritual sacrifices, and demonstrate God's love in practical ways. Your life is a reflection of God's holiness, and your actions and prayers can help bring others closer to Him.

Live Out Your Calling

Living out your calling as a king and priest requires daily dedication and faithfulness. It involves not only personal transformation but also active engagement with the world around you. Here are some ways to live out this calling:

- Walk in Holiness: As a priest, your life is meant to reflect the holiness of God. Pursue purity, avoid sin, and rely on the Holy Spirit to guide your steps. You are called to be set apart in your conduct, honoring God in everything you do.

- Exercise Spiritual Authority: As a king, you are called to bring the rule and reign of God into your circumstances. Pray with confidence, stand against the works of darkness, and steward the gifts and resources God has given you for His glory.

- Serve with Compassion: Part of your priestly role is to serve others with love, humility, and compassion. Whether through acts of kindness, words of encouragement, or offering support in times of need, your service is a reflection of Christ's love for the world.

- Proclaim the Gospel: One of the primary responsibilities of the royal priesthood is to declare the praises of God and share the good news of salvation. Look for opportunities to share your faith with others, whether through your words, your actions, or your testimony of God's work in your life.

Rely on God's Grace and Power

While the calling to live as kings and priests is a high one, it is not one that you are expected to fulfill in your own strength. God's grace and power are available to you every step of the way. 2 Corinthians 12:9 reminds us, "My grace is sufficient for you, for My power is made perfect in weakness." As you rely on God's strength:

- Trust in His Grace: God's grace is what empowers you to live out your calling. Even when you fall short, His grace is there to lift you up and help you continue in your journey of faith. You are not defined by your mistakes but by the grace of God that covers you and makes you whole.

- Lean on His Power: The Holy Spirit is your constant source of power. He equips you with spiritual gifts, strengthens you in times of weakness, and enables you to walk in victory over sin and challenges. Depend on the Spirit's leading and empowerment in all that you do.

- Persevere in Hope: The journey of faith is not always easy, but you can persevere knowing that God's promises are true. The eternal kingdom awaits, and your faithful service on earth has eternal significance. Keep your eyes fixed on Christ, knowing that He will give you the strength to endure and the reward of reigning with Him.

Closing Encouragement

Believers, you are kings and priests in God's eternal kingdom. Embrace this identity fully, live out your calling with passion and purpose, and rely on God's grace and power to guide you in every step. The path of a king and priest is one of service, authority, and holiness, and it leads to eternal glory with Christ. As you continue in your journey, know that you are never alone—God is with you, empowering you, and working through you to bring about His kingdom on earth as it is in heaven.

CALL TO EMBRACE THE IDENTITY

As this book concludes, the final call is for every believer to fully embrace their God-given identity as kings and priests, stepping confidently into the roles for which they have been chosen. This is not merely a symbolic title but a profound truth that defines the life, purpose, and mission of every follower of Christ. Understanding and walking in this identity allows believers to fulfill their part in God's redemptive plan and to experience the fullness of what it means to be His people.

Step Into Your Role as Kings

As kings in God's kingdom, you have been given authority through Christ to stand firm, exercise dominion over sin, and bring the rule and reign of God into the world around you. The calling to kingship is one of leadership, stewardship, and influence—not for personal gain, but for the glory of God and the advancement of His kingdom. You are called to lead with integrity, live with purpose, and confront the forces of darkness with the light of Christ.

- Walk in Confidence: God has equipped you with spiritual authority to overcome challenges, resist the enemy, and bring His justice and righteousness into every situation. As you walk in this role, you reflect the victory that Christ has already won on the cross.

- Steward God's Gifts: Everything you have—your time, talents, and resources—has been entrusted to you by God. As a king, your role is to steward these gifts wisely, using them to build up the kingdom of God and serve others in love.

- Influence for His Kingdom: Your influence extends beyond the walls of the church; it touches every aspect of life—your family, work, community, and beyond. As a representative of Christ's kingdom, you are called to shine His light and extend His grace wherever you go.

Embrace Your Role as Priests

As priests, you have the privilege of worshiping God, interceding for others, and offering spiritual sacrifices that are pleasing to Him. The priestly calling is one of holiness, service, and mediation, representing God's heart to the world and drawing others into His presence.

- Live in Holiness: You are set apart for God's purposes. As a priest, you are called to live a life of purity and devotion, reflecting the holiness of God in all that you do.

Through prayer, worship, and obedience, you fulfill your priestly duty of drawing near to God.

- Serve Others: As a priest, you are called to intercede for others, stand in the gap, and serve those in need. Your prayers and acts of service are powerful, helping to bring about God's will and leading others into a deeper relationship with Him.

- Worship in Spirit and Truth: Your life is a living sacrifice, an offering of worship to God. Whether in prayer, praise, or action, your priestly role is to worship God with your whole being, bringing glory to His name and inviting others to do the same.

A Call to Confidence and Dedication

This is a call to confidence and dedication. The identity of kings and priests is not something to be taken lightly—it is a holy calling that demands commitment, but it also comes with the assurance of God's grace and power. As you step into your role, you do so knowing that God is with you, enabling you to fulfill His purposes.

- Confidence in God's Calling: Your identity as a king and priest has been given to you by God Himself. You did not earn it, but through Christ, you have been made worthy to carry out this calling. Walk boldly in the knowledge that God has chosen you and empowered you for this purpose.

- Dedication to His Mission: Embracing your role as king and priest means dedicating yourself to the mission of God's kingdom. It means serving others, standing for truth, living in holiness, and leading with love. It means being faithful to the calling, knowing that your labor is not in vain and that God's eternal kingdom is your ultimate reward.

Embrace Your Identity

Believers, the time has come to fully embrace your identity as kings and priests. You are part of a royal priesthood, a holy nation, and a people set apart for God's glory. Step into your calling with confidence, live out your purpose with dedication, and rely on the power of God to guide and strengthen you on this journey.

As you walk in this identity, you will not only experience the fullness of God's presence in your own life, but you will also impact the world around you, bringing the light of Christ into every dark corner and advancing the kingdom of God on earth.

You are kings and priests—now go and live as those who have been called, chosen, and empowered for such a time as this.

APPENDICES

Relevant Bible Verses

This compilation of key Bible verses related to the themes of kingship and priesthood provides a rich resource for further study, reflection, and understanding of the profound identity and calling that believers hold in Christ. These verses help to deepen the biblical foundation of believers as kings and priests, exploring how this identity is revealed throughout Scripture and how it shapes the life and mission of God's people.

Kingship Verses

1. Genesis 1:26-28

"Then God said, 'Let Us make mankind in Our image, in Our likeness, so that they may rule over the fish in the sea and the birds in the sky, over the livestock and all the wild animals, and over all the creatures that move along the ground.' So God created mankind in His own image, in the image of God He created them; male and female He created them. God blessed them and said to them, 'Be fruitful and increase in number; fill the earth and subdue it. Rule over the fish in the sea and the birds in the sky and over every living creature that moves on the ground.'"

This foundational verse reveals God's original intention for humanity—to rule over creation as His representatives, reflecting His authority and stewardship.

2. Revelation 1:6

"And has made us kings and priests to His God and Father, to Him be glory and dominion forever and ever. Amen."

This verse highlights the dual identity of believers as kings and priests, emphasizing the authority given to believers through Christ to rule and serve God.

3. Revelation 5:10

"And have made us kings and priests to our God; and we shall reign on the earth."

A confirmation of the eternal role of believers in reigning with Christ over the new earth, sharing in His authority as His co-heirs.

4. 2 Timothy 2:12

"If we endure, we will also reign with Him. If we disown Him, He will also disown us."

This verse affirms the promise that those who faithfully follow Christ and endure in their faith will reign with Him in His kingdom.

5. Romans 8:17

"Now if we are children, then we are heirs—heirs of God and co-heirs with Christ, if indeed we share in His sufferings in order that we may also share in His glory."

Believers are described as co-heirs with Christ, sharing in His suffering and His glory, which includes ruling with Him in the future kingdom.

6. Matthew 25:34

"Then the King will say to those on His right, 'Come, you who are blessed by My Father; take your inheritance, the kingdom prepared for you since the creation of the world.'"

This verse speaks to the inheritance awaiting believers, a kingdom prepared for them by God from the very beginning of time.

7. Psalm 2:6-8

"I have installed My king on Zion, My holy mountain. I will proclaim the Lord's decree: He said to Me, 'You are My son; today I have become your Father. Ask Me, and I will make the nations your inheritance, the ends of the earth your possession.'"

A prophetic passage revealing the kingship of Christ, which believers will share in as His co-heirs.

8. Revelation 22:5

"There will be no more night. They will not need the light of a lamp or the light of the sun, for the Lord God will give them light. And they will reign for ever and ever."

The eternal reign of believers is confirmed in this passage, pointing to the everlasting nature of their kingship in the presence of God.

Priesthood Verses

1. Exodus 19:6

"You will be for Me a kingdom of priests and a holy nation. These are the words you are to speak to the Israelites."

God's original calling to the people of Israel to be a kingdom of priests and a holy nation, a role that is fulfilled in the church through Christ.

2. 1 Peter 2:9

"But you are a chosen people, a royal priesthood, a holy nation, God's special possession, that you may declare the praises of Him who called you out of darkness into His wonderful light."

A key New Testament verse that reaffirms the church's identity as a royal priesthood, set apart to declare God's praises and reflect His glory.

3. Revelation 1:6

"And has made us kings and priests to His God and Father, to Him be glory and dominion forever and ever. Amen."

Again, this verse highlights the priestly identity of believers, emphasizing their role in serving God.

4. Revelation 20:6

"Blessed and holy are those who share in the first resurrection. The second death has no power over them, but they will be priests of God and of Christ and will reign with Him for a thousand years."

A promise that those who belong to Christ will serve as priests in the millennium, reigning with Him.

5. Hebrews 4:14-16

"Therefore, since we have a great high priest who has ascended into heaven, Jesus the Son of God, let us hold firmly to the faith we profess. For we do not have a high priest who is unable to empathize with our weaknesses, but we have one who has been tempted in every way, just as we are—yet He did not sin. Let us then approach God's throne of grace with confidence, so that we may receive mercy and find grace to help us in our time of need."

This passage connects believers' priestly identity with Christ's high priesthood, encouraging them to approach God confidently and intercede for others.

6. Romans 12:1

"Therefore, I urge you, brothers and sisters, in view of God's mercy, to offer your bodies as a living sacrifice, holy and pleasing to God—this is your true and proper worship."

As priests, believers are called to offer themselves as living sacrifices, worshiping God through holy and obedient lives.

7. 1 Samuel 2:35

"I will raise up for Myself a faithful priest, who will do according to what is in My heart and mind. I will firmly establish his priestly house, and they will minister before My anointed one always."

A prophetic promise of a faithful priesthood, ultimately fulfilled in Christ and those who serve under His priesthood.

8. Hebrews 13:15-16

"Through Jesus, therefore, let us continually offer to God a sacrifice of praise—the fruit of lips that openly profess His name. And do not forget to do good and to share with others, for with such sacrifices God is pleased."

This verse encourages believers to live out their priestly role through praise, good deeds, and generosity, offering spiritual sacrifices pleasing to God.

Verses on the Eternal Kingdom

1. Revelation 21:1-3

"Then I saw 'a new heaven and a new earth,' for the first heaven and the first earth had passed away, and there was no longer any sea. I saw the Holy City, the new Jerusalem, coming down out of heaven from God, prepared as a bride beautifully dressed for her husband. And I heard a loud voice from the throne saying, 'Look! God's dwelling place is now among the people, and He will dwell with them. They will be His people, and God Himself will be with them and be their God.'"

This passage presents the ultimate promise of the new heaven and new earth, where believers will dwell with God for eternity.

2. Isaiah 65:17

"See, I will create new heavens and a new earth. The former things will not be remembered, nor will they come to mind."

Isaiah prophesies the creation of the new heaven and new earth, a place of peace and restoration where the old order of things has passed away.

3. Revelation 22:3-5

"No longer will there be any curse. The throne of God and of the Lamb will be in the city, and His servants will serve Him. They will see His face, and His name will be on their foreheads. There will be no more night. They will not need the light of a lamp or the light of the sun, for the Lord God will give them light. And they will reign for ever and ever."

This verse describes the eternal reign of believers in the new heaven and new earth, where they will serve God and enjoy the fullness of His presence.

These verses provide a comprehensive biblical framework for understanding the royal priesthood of believers, their calling as kings and priests, and the glorious hope of eternity in the presence of God. Use these Scriptures for study, reflection, and prayer as you continue to explore and embrace your identity in Christ.

STUDY QUESTIONS FOR GROUP DISCUSSION

These questions are designed to facilitate group discussion and encourage deeper understanding and personal reflection on the themes presented in this book. Whether used in a small group setting, Bible study, or personal study, these questions will help participants explore the profound identity of believers as kings and priests and how this impacts their lives and calling.

Chapter 1: Biblical Foundation of Kings and Priests

1. How does Revelation 1:6 and Exodus 19:6 shape your understanding of your identity as a king and priest?

2. In what ways does knowing you are part of a "royal priesthood" (1 Peter 2:9) change the way you view your daily life and responsibilities?

3. How does the Old Testament concept of kingship and priesthood point to the work of Christ? How does it relate to the church today?

Chapter 2: Historical Context of Kings and Priests in Ancient Israel

1. What were the primary roles of kings and priests in ancient Israel, and how did they serve God's purposes?

2. How did the intersection of kingship and priesthood in figures like David and Melchizedek foreshadow Christ's ultimate role as King and High Priest?

3. How do the failures of Israel's kings and priests remind us of the need for Christ's perfect kingship and priesthood?

Chapter 3: Jesus Christ – The Ultimate King and Priest

1. How does Jesus perfectly fulfill the roles of both King and Priest? In what ways do you experience His kingship and priesthood in your own life?

2. What does the Melchizedek connection (Hebrews 7) teach us about the eternal nature of Christ's priesthood?

3. In what areas of your life do you need to submit to Christ's kingship? How can you better embrace His role as your High Priest, particularly in times of need?

Chapter 4: The New Covenant and the Believer's Role

1. How does the New Covenant shift the roles of kingship and priesthood from the Old Testament to the church? What are the key differences?

2. How can you exercise your spiritual authority as a king in Christ? What does this look like in practical terms in your everyday life?

3. How are you currently fulfilling your responsibility as a priest through prayer, worship, and service? What areas might you need to grow in?

Chapter 5: Living as Kings and Priests Today

1. How do you see the spiritual battles you face as part of your kingship? How can you be better equipped to fight these battles through prayer and the Word of God?

2. How does the role of a priest as an intercessor affect how you pray for others? How can you become more intentional in your priestly ministry of prayer?

3. What does holiness look like in your life today? How can you pursue greater purity in your thoughts, words, and actions as a priest of God?

Chapter 6: The Church as a Royal Priesthood

1. In what ways does the corporate identity of the church as a royal priesthood impact the church's mission and purpose in the world?

2. How does your understanding of your personal identity as a king and priest affect your role within the local church community?

3. How can the church more effectively fulfill its mission of declaring God's praises and advancing His kingdom on earth?

Chapter 7: Practical Application in Daily Life

1. How can you lead with integrity and wisdom as a king in your family, workplace, or community?

2. What are practical ways you can serve with compassion and humility as a priest, especially to those in need around you?

3. How are you currently declaring God's praises in your life? How can you be more intentional about sharing your testimony and the gospel with others?

Chapter 8: The Eternal Kingdom

1. How does the promise of the new heaven and new earth give you hope in the face of life's challenges?

2. How does knowing you will reign with Christ in eternity affect how you live today? How can you live with an eternal perspective, especially in difficult times?

3. What does it mean to serve God as a priest in the eternal kingdom? How can you prepare now for this future role?

Chapter 9: Persevering with Hope

1. How does 2 Corinthians 4:17-18 encourage you to persevere through difficult times? How can you remind yourself to focus on the unseen, eternal reality?

2. What are some specific challenges you are facing right now where you need to draw on the hope of your future kingship and priesthood in Christ?

3. How can the church better support each other in persevering through trials, knowing that we will one day reign with Christ?

Chapter 10: Our Eternal Role as Kings and Priests

1. What excites you most about the idea of reigning and serving with Christ in the new heaven and new earth?

2. How does this eternal calling shape your understanding of your current responsibilities as a king and priest?

3. In what ways can you start living out your eternal role now, in your worship, service, and leadership?

Call to Embrace the Identity

1. What steps can you take this week to fully embrace your identity as a king and priest in God's kingdom?

2. What are the areas of your life where you need to grow in confidence and dedication in fulfilling your role?

3. How can you rely more on God's grace and power as you seek to walk in your identity as a royal priesthood?

1. After reflecting on the entire book, what is the most impactful truth you have learned about your identity as a king and priest?

2. How will you take what you have learned and apply it to your daily walk with God, your relationship with others, and your mission in the world?

3. In what ways can you encourage others to embrace their own God-given identity as part of the royal priesthood?

These questions are intended to spark deep discussion, personal reflection, and spiritual growth, allowing each participant to consider the profound significance of their identity as kings and priests and to apply these truths to their lives.

Prayers for Kings and Priests

These sample prayers are designed to help believers seek God's guidance, strength, and empowerment as they live out their calling as kings and priests in His kingdom. Through these prayers, believers can ask God to help them walk in their divine identity, serve with humility, and reign with spiritual authority, all while bringing glory to His name.

1. Prayer for Embracing Identity as Kings and Priests

Heavenly Father,

Thank You for calling me to be part of Your royal priesthood. I am humbled and grateful that You have chosen me to be both a king and a priest in Your kingdom. Help me to fully embrace this identity, not with pride, but with a heart of humility and service. Show me how to walk confidently in the authority You have given me as a king and how to serve with love and dedication as a priest.

Teach me to reflect Your holiness in all that I do, to lead with wisdom, and to serve others with compassion. Empower me to carry out Your will, both in my life and in the world around me. I trust in Your grace and strength to guide me every step of the way.

In Jesus' name,

Amen.

2. Prayer for Spiritual Authority as a King

Lord Jesus, King of Kings,

I praise You for making me a part of Your kingdom and for entrusting me with spiritual authority. Help me to live as a faithful king under Your lordship. Teach me how to exercise this authority in ways that reflect Your justice, mercy, and love. Guide me in using the power of prayer, Your Word, and the Holy Spirit to overcome sin, resist the works of the enemy, and bring Your light into dark places.

Give me wisdom in leading those around me, whether in my family, workplace, or community. Help me to make decisions that align with Your will, to act with integrity, and to influence others for Your kingdom. Strengthen me to stand firm in faith and to advance Your kingdom on earth.

I pray all of this in Your mighty name, Jesus,

Amen.

3. Prayer for Holiness and Service as a Priest

Gracious Father,

You have called me to be a priest in Your kingdom, to live a life of holiness and service. I come before You today, asking for Your grace to walk in purity, integrity, and devotion to You. Purify my heart, mind, and actions so that my life would be a reflection of Your holiness and love.

Help me to serve others with humility and compassion, just as Jesus served us. Give me a heart that seeks to intercede for those in need, to offer prayers for healing, comfort, and salvation. May my worship be pleasing to You, not only in song and prayer but in every act of love and kindness that I offer in Your name.

Empower me to live as a faithful priest, serving Your people and drawing others closer to You. Let my life be a living sacrifice, holy and acceptable to You.

In Jesus' name,

Amen.

4. Prayer for Strength in Spiritual Battles

Almighty God,

As a king in Your kingdom, I know that I am called to engage in spiritual battles. I come to You now, seeking Your strength and protection. Equip me with the full armor of God so that I may stand firm against the schemes of the enemy. Help me to fight with the power of Your Word and the truth of Your promises.

When I feel weak, remind me that Your strength is made perfect in my weakness. When I face challenges, help me to keep my eyes fixed on You, knowing that You have already won the victory. Give me the courage to stand firm in the face of opposition, to resist temptation, and to advance Your kingdom through prayer and faithful living.

I place my trust in You, Lord, as my protector and defender. Empower me to walk in victory, not by my own strength, but by the power of Your Holy Spirit.

In Jesus' powerful name,

Amen.

5. Prayer for Wisdom and Integrity in Leadership

Lord God,

You have called me to lead as a king in Your kingdom, and I ask for Your wisdom and guidance as I take on this responsibility. Help me to lead with integrity, always seeking to do what is right in Your sight. Give me the discernment to make decisions that align with Your will and reflect Your character.

In every situation, help me to lead by example, showing love, humility, and grace to those around me. May I be a reflection of Christ's leadership, leading not with pride, but with a servant's heart. Empower me to be a source of encouragement and strength for others, always pointing them toward You.

Help me to steward the gifts and resources You have given me wisely, using them to build up Your kingdom and serve others. May my leadership bring glory to Your name and advance Your purposes on earth.

In Jesus' name,

Amen.

6. Prayer for Intercession and Compassion

Father in Heaven,

As a priest in Your kingdom, You have called me to be an intercessor for others. I come before You today, lifting up those who are in need of Your grace, healing, and comfort. Use me as a vessel of Your compassion, that I may stand in the gap for others through prayer and service.

Give me a heart that is sensitive to the needs of those around me. Help me to pray for others with faith, trusting that

You hear every word and are working in their lives. Give me the courage to intercede for those who are lost, broken, or hurting, and to trust in Your power to bring about transformation.

Help me to love others as You love them, and may my life be a reflection of Your compassion and mercy.

In Jesus' name,

Amen.

7. Prayer for Perseverance and Hope

Heavenly Father,

In moments of trial and difficulty, remind me of the eternal hope I have as a king and priest in Your kingdom. When I feel weary, give me the strength to persevere, knowing that You have called me to reign with Christ and serve You for eternity. Help me to keep my eyes on the unseen, eternal promises of Your kingdom, even when the challenges of this world seem overwhelming.

Thank You for the hope I have in You, the assurance that my present trials are temporary and that You are with me through every storm. Strengthen me to endure, to trust in Your plan, and to walk faithfully in my calling as Your servant.

I look forward with hope to the day when I will reign with You in the new heaven and new earth. Until that day, help me to live with faith, perseverance, and joy, knowing that my future is secure in Christ.

In Jesus' name,

Amen.

8. Prayer for Unity in the Royal Priesthood

Lord,

You have called Your church to be a royal priesthood, a community of believers united in purpose and mission. I pray for unity among Your people, that we may work together to declare Your praises and advance Your kingdom on earth. Help us to support one another, to pray for one another, and to serve each other in love.

Bind us together with the bond of peace, and may our unity reflect the love and oneness of Christ. As we walk in our identity as kings and priests, may we do so with humility, knowing that we are all part of one body, called to serve the same Lord.

May Your church be a shining example of love, unity, and grace in the world, drawing others to You through our witness.

In Jesus' name,

Amen.

These prayers are meant to guide you as you live out your royal priesthood. As you pray them, invite the Holy Spirit to shape your heart, empower your service, and help you walk confidently in the identity God has given you as a king and priest in His eternal kingdom.